Tefilin

A CHASSIDIC DISCOURSE

by Rabbi Nathan of Breslov

Likutey Halachot, Hilchot Tefilin 5:

A free rendition by Avraham Greenbaum

PUBLISHED BY
THE BRESLOV RESEARCH INSTITUTE

הספר הקדוש הזה נדפס לעילוי נשמת

ר׳ **נפתלי דוד** ב״ר **בנימין** ז״ל

נפ׳ כ״א אדר א׳ תשמ״ו

על ידי בנו

ר׳ **אריה ליב משה** ב״ר **נפתלי דוד ספירו** נ״י

In loving memory of my dear father

Nelson (Dave) Spiro z'l

(d. 21st Adar I 5746 - 1st March 1986)

Who prayed with Tefilin all his life.

Aryeh Lev Moshe Spiro

INTRODUCTION

It's hard to be enthusiastic about doing something if you don't understand the value of what you're doing. Practical religious observance in all spheres of life is the very essence of Judaism. But without an understanding of the inner meaning and intention — the *kavanah* — of Jewish practice, it easily becomes like a body without a soul. What is the connection between the details of practical observance and the quest for spirituality?

That is precisely the link that Rabbi Nathan (1780-1844) — closest pupil of the Chassidic Master, Rebbe Nachman of Breslov — sought to trace in the eight volumes of his *Likutey Halachot* ("Collected Laws"). This work is a comprehensive survey of the entire body of Jewish Law applicable today, as codified in the *Shulchan Aruch* and following its order subject by subject. On each subject Rabbi Nathan wrote several ma'marim — discourses or essays — of varying length. In them he illuminates the spiritual and mystical significance of all the different areas of Jewish practice in the light of the insights of Chassidic teaching, especially the teachings of Rebbe Nachman in his *Likutey Moharan* and elsewhere.

At a time of spiritual awakening for Jews all over the world, Likutey Halachot could prove to be one of our most important and relevant texts. Rebbe Nachman once praised Rabbi Nathan as having the gift of being able to "explain the profound secrets of mysticism to little Jewish children"! The discourses in Likutey Halachot are written in a clear, easily intelligible style. Ranging over the entire TaNaCh, Talmud, Midrash, Zohar etc. they open up deeply fascinating vistas in the meaning of all aspects of Judaism and life.

The present work is a free rendition of the greater part of just one ma'amar from Likutey Halachot, on the subject of Tefilin. The ma'amar appears in Likutey Halachot, Orach Chaim, Hilchot Tefilin 5. Rabbi Nathan takes as his starting point Rebbe Nachman's story of the Blind Beggar (which has been printed here in full for convenience.) This story is one of the six sub-stories making up the Tale of the Seven Beggars, which is the last, the most extensive, and perhaps the most mysterious of all of Rebbe Nachman's tales.

On the surface the story of the Blind Beggar appears to make no reference to Tefilin at all. Yet in a masterful tour-de-force Rabbi Nathan shows that the story is in fact alive with powerful and vivid allusions to the deepest *kavanot* of the mitzva of Tefilin. Alive is the word, because vitality and renewal are the key ideas in Rabbi Nathan's exploration of the different facets of the Tefilin. With references to other relevant teachings of Rebbe Nachman, and to the main Biblical, Talmudic, Halachic and Kabbalistic sources, Rabbi Nathan takes us through virtually every aspect of the mitzva of Tefilin: the Tefilin of the head and the hand; the Torah portions (*parshiyot*), the capsules (*batim*), the straps (*retzu'ot*), the knots (*kesharim*), the materials (parchment and leather), Rashi and Rabbenu Tam Tefilin, etc.

Rabbi Nathan's teachings are *Chidushey Torah* — original Torah insights — in the true sense of the term. Without adding personal and subjective interpretations having no basis in the classic sources, Rabbi Nathan uncovers a wealth of fresh perspectives; he clarifies the connections between many different Torah concepts; and he gives us a grasp of deeper meanings in understandable and relevant terms with such ease that we may hardly be aware of what he is doing with us! Yet his purpose is far from being just to take us on an exciting intellectual journey. For "the main thing is not study but practice" (Avot 1:17). If Rabbi Nathan treats us to an array of spiritual delicacies, it is to encourage us on our way, to inspire us to action and achievement, and to offer practical guidance as to how to go about our search for God.

In this, Rabbi Nathan is a true student of his master, Rebbe Nachman. In his own discourses, talks and stories, Rebbe Nachman provided the seminal ideas. However their light is so concentrated that they often appear enigmatic and obscure. Rebbe Nachman said that all his teachings are "introductions" and that they can be applied to the whole written and oral Torah (Rabbi Nachman's Wisdom #200 & #201). The work of Rabbi Nathan, who knew the Rebbe more closely than anybody and was in the best position to understand his intentions, was to draw out the corollaries — as we see him do here in taking the Story of the Blind Beggar and other teachings to throw light on the meaning of the Tefilin.

Rebbe Nachman once remarked of R. Nathan that "he would just have to glance at this synagogue and he could tell you how many feet high it is" (Tzaddik #338). This remark vividly depicts the distinctive quality of Rabbi Nathan's mind: he had the ability to grasp a whole and all its constituent parts at one and the same time.

This is evident in the way Rabbi Nathan's ma'morim are structured. On a casual reading their flow from one subject to another, and another, and so on, can make them seem diffuse, while the repeated references to certain basic ideas and connections may appear labored. Deeper study reveals the magnificent edifice R. Nathan is patiently building — with each chamber, each subsection, beautifully proportioned and decorated, while all are held together in a firm, harmonious structure with connecting beams and girders — the basic ideas. If the ideas are sometimes repeated, the purpose is to keep us aware of the whole as we are shown all the various parts.   Rabbi Nathan frequently connects a variety of substructures to his main structure, digressing from his initial theme to show how the ideas he is presenting illumine related areas of Torah. A few such sections in the present ma'mor on Tefilin have been left out of this edition, since it would otherwise have outgrown the booklet format. The section numbers in this edition correspond to those in the Hebrew original, and thus a gap in the sequence of section numbers indicates that a section has been omitted. In addition, it seemed that in some places Rabbi Nathan's repetition of basic ideas (which is more concise in Hebrew than when translated in English) might become somewhat burdensome to contemporary readers, and a number of such passages have been abbreviated.

The aim has been to present an English version that is fully faithful to the intent and spirit of the original, while being as readable as Rabbi Nathan's Hebrew is. This meant diverging frequently from literal translation, which is why this work is described as a "free rendition". In many places extra explanatory information has been worked into the fabric of the text to avoid having to distract the reader with footnotes. Where lengthier explanations of some of the underlying concepts have been introduced, they have been printed in italics or square brackets to indicate that they are translator's additions.

I am grateful to God for giving me the privilege of translating this ma'mor: it has touched me in so many ways and added entirely new dimensions to my understanding and fulfilment of the mitzva of Tefilin. The debt I owe to Rabbi Chaim Kramer, Director of the Breslov Research Institute, is immeasurable. In this, as in every project, he has given encouragement and unstinting practical help at every step of the way. I would also like to express my sincere thanks to Aryeh Leib (Larry) Spiro, whose support enabled me to first start serious work on this book.

And finally, I must express my deepest appreciation and gratitude to Chaim Rohatiner, whose outstanding contribution made it possible to continue with the work and bring the entire project to completion. Your proven friendship, offered with unfailing kindness and good humor, has touched me very profoundly, while your persistence and devotion to Breslover Chassidus have been a real inspiration.

So far only a handful of extracts from Likutey Halachot have appeared in English: the living spring of Rabbi Nathan's Torah has hardly begun to be tapped. The ma'mor on Tefilin presented here is fascinating and powerfully inspiring in itself. It is my hope and prayer that its publication will arouse English-speaking Jewry to a greater awareness of the importance of Likutey Halachot, and open the way to many further translations, until "the world is full of the knowledge of G-d as the waters cover the sea" (Isaiah 11:9).

Avraham Greenbaum
Jerusalem, 25th Kislev 5749
4th December '88

1. The Arm Tefilin

(a) The Arm Tefilin in place on the biceps, showing the customary seven windings of the *retzu'a* on the lower arm, and the windings of the *retzu'a* around the third finger and the hand to form the Divine name *Shaddai*.

(b) The *bayit* of the Arm Tefilin, made up of a single compartment, showing the *retzu'a*, the strap, running through the *ma'barta*, and the loop of the *retzu'a* by means of which the Tefilin is bound to the arm. Right next to the *bayit* is the *kesher*, the knot, tied in the shape of the letter *Yod*. The stitches of animal sinew thread with which the *bayit* is sewn closed after insertion of the *parshiyot* can be seen running around the top of the base.

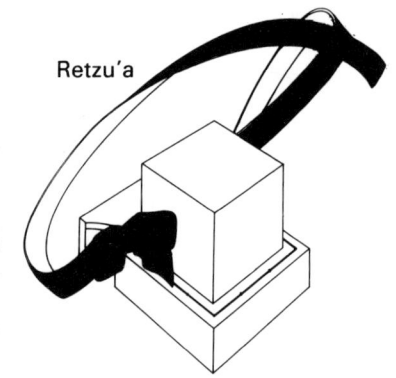

Retzu'a

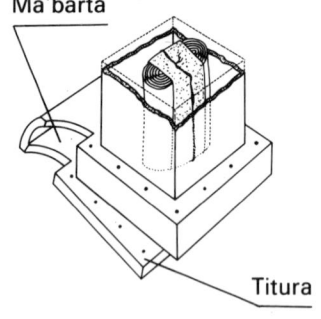

Ma'barta

Titura

(c) The *bayit* of the Arm Tefilin showing the *titura* hanging open as it would be in order to insert the *par'shiyot*. The *parshiyot* are visible in place inside. The four *parshiyot* of the Arm Tefilin are written on a single slip of parchment. This is then rolled up and tied around with a thread of animal sinew, wrapped around with a narrow slip of parchment, and tied around on the outside with thread of animal sinew.

THE LAWS OF TEFILIN

"Bind them for a sign on your arm, and let them be as ornaments between your eyes." (Deuteronomy 6:8)

This verse gives the commandment to wear Tefilin. The Tefilin consist of cube-shaped capsules (in Hebrew, *batim*, literally "houses") made of leather from a ritually pure animal, such as an ox, sheep or deer. These capsules contain four Biblical passages (the *parshiyot*) hand-written on parchment. The passages are A. "Sanctify" (Exodus 13:1-10); B. "When God will bring you" (Exodus 13:11-16); C. "Shema" (Deuteronomy 6:4-9); and D. "If you will listen" (Deuteronomy 11:13-21). (These passages are printed in full below.) The capsules are painted black. The underside of each capsule is covered with a flap of leather (the *titura*) and the capsules are sewn closed with threads made of animal sinews.

The Tefilin are placed on the head and the arm. The main difference between the Tefilin of the head and those of the arm is that in the Head Tefilin the four Biblical passages are written on four separate slips of parchment, each of which is contained in its own narrow compartment, the four compartments together making up the cube. In the Hand Tefilin, however, all four passages are written on one piece of parchment inserted into a single compartment.

The mitzva is to bind the Tefilin on the biceps of the left arm (a left-handed person binds them on his right arm) and on the top of the head, between the hairline and the spot where an infant's head is soft, in a direct line above the

2. The Head Tefilin

(a) The Head Tefilin held in place by the *retzu'a*. The *bayit* is in its correct position on the top of the head, with the *kesher*, the knot, in its correct position at the back of the head where the neck meets the base of the skull. The two ends of the *retzu'a* hang down in front, reaching to at least the navel on the right side of the wearer and his chest on the left.

Kesher

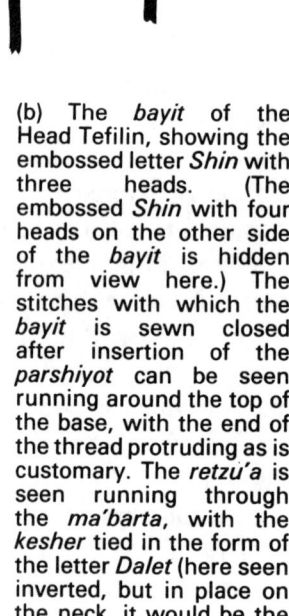

Ma'barta

(b) The *bayit* of the Head Tefilin, showing the embossed letter *Shin* with three heads. (The embossed *Shin* with four heads on the other side of the *bayit* is hidden from view here.) The stitches with which the *bayit* is sewn closed after insertion of the *parshiyot* can be seen running around the top of the base, with the end of the thread protruding as is customary. The *retzu'a* is seen running through the *ma'barta*, with the *kesher* tied in the form of the letter *Dalet* (here seen inverted, but in place on the neck, it would be the right way up).

mid-point between the eyes. The Tefilin are attached to the arm and head with black leather straps about a centimeter or more in width — the *retzu'ot* (singular *retzu'a*). These straps run through passageways formed at the lower edges of each of the *batim* where the flap (the *titura*) folds over to cover the underside of the compartment. The passage is called the *ma'abarta*, literally "the crossing". The *retzu'ot* of the Head and Arm Tefilin each have their distinctive knots in the shape of the Hebrew letters Dalet and Yod respectively.

Order of Putting on the Tefilin

The Tefilin are worn by Jewish males over the age of thirteen during the weekday morning prayer-service, but not on Shabbat or the major Festivals. It is forbidden to show disrespect for the Tefilin by wearing them in an unclean place (bathroom etc.) or before attending to one's bodily needs.

After putting on the Tallit (prayer-shawl), the Arm Tefilin is placed over the biceps, after which the blessing is recited. The strap is then immediately tightened to hold the compartment firmly in place on the arm. The strap is next wound around the lower arm seven times, after which it is temporarily wound loosely around the hand.

The Head Tefilin is now put in place, and its appropriate blessing is recited silently, after which the strap is positioned firmly around the skull with the knot at the back of the head where the neck meets the base of the skull, and some verses are recited.

The end of the arm strap, which had been temporarily wound around the hand, is taken off the hand. It is then wound three times around the third finger and around the palm of the hand in such a way as to form the Hebrew letters making up the Divine Name, "Shaddai" (except when praying, we avoid pronouncing this Name as spelled and say it as "Shakkai").

The *Parshiyot*

A. Exodus 13:1-10:

And God spoke to Moses saying. Sanctify to Me every firstborn: the first issue of every womb among the Children of Israel, both of man and of beast, is Mine. And Moses said to the people: Remember this day on which you went out from Egypt, from the house of bondage, for God took you out of here with a strong hand, and no chametz may be eaten. Today you are leaving, in the month of Aviv. And it will come to pass, when God will bring you to the land of the Canaanites, the Hittites, the Emorites, the Hivvites and the Jebusites, which He swore to your fathers to give you — a land flowing with milk and honey — that you shall perform this service in this month. For seven days eat matzot, and on the seventh day there shall be a festival to God. Matzot shall be eaten for seven days, and let no chametz be seen in your possession, and let no leaven be seen in your possesion in all your borders. And tell your son on that day, saying, "Because of this God acted on my behalf when I left Egypt." And it shall be for you as a sign on your arm and as a reminder between your eyes — in order that God's Torah may be in your mouth, for with a strong hand God brought you out from Egypt. And you shall observe this ordinance at its designated time from year to year.

B. Exodus 13:11-16:

And it shall come to pass, when God will bring you to the land of the Canaanites, as He swore to you and your fathers, and will have given it to you. You shall set aside every first issue of the womb for God, and every first issue that is brought forth by cattle that belong to you, the males will be for God. And every first issue of a donkey you shall redeem with a lamb or a kid, and if you do not redeem it then you must break its neck, and every human firstborn among your sons you must redeem. And when your son asks you in the future, saying "What is this?" you shall say to him, "With a strong hand God took us out of Egypt, out of the house of bondage. And when Pharaoh stubbornly refused to send us away, God killed every firstborn in the land of Egypt, from the firstborn of humans to the firstborn of the animals. This is why I sacrifice to God every first male issue of the womb, and every firstborn of my sons I redeem." And it shall be for a sign on your hand and for frontlets between your eyes, for God took us out of Egypt with a strong hand.

C. Deuteronomy 6:4-9:

Hear O Israel, HaShem is our God, HaShem is one. And you shall love HaShem your God with all your heart and with all your soul and with all your might. And these words which I command you this day shall be on your heart. And you shall ingrain them in your children and speak of them when you sit in your house and when you go on your way and when you lie down and when you get up. And you shall bind them for a sign on your arm and they shall be for frontlets between your eyes. And you shall write them on the doorposts of your house and on your gates.

D. Deuteronomy 11:13-21:

And it shall be if you will listen carefully to My commandments which I am commanding you today, to love HaShem your God and to serve Him with all your hearts and all your souls. And I will give the rain of your land in its season, the early and the late rains, and you will gather in your grain and your wine and your oil. And I will give grass in your field for your catle, and you will eat and be satisfied. Be on your guard in case your heart is seduced and you turn aside and serve other gods and bow down to them. Then God's anger will burn against you and He will close up the heavens and there will be no rain, and the ground will not yield its produce, and you will soon be banished from the good land that God is giving you. So put these words of Mine on your heart and on your soul, and bind them for a sign on your hand, and let them be for frontlets between your eyes. And teach them to your children to speak of them when you sit in your house and when you go on your way, when you lie down and when you rise up. And write them on the doorposts of your house and on your gates, in order that your days and the days of your children should be many on the land which God swore to your fathers to give them like the days of the heavens on the earth.

*

THE BLIND BEGGAR

The Story of the Blind Beggar is one of the sub-stories in Rabbi Nachman's Tale of the Seven Beggars, which has been translated in full in "Rabbi Nachman's Stories" by Rabbi Aryeh Kaplan (Breslov Research Institute 1983) pp.354- 437.

One day there was a mass flight from a certain country, in the course of which a young boy and girl got lost in the forest. They had no food and began screaming and crying, when suddenly a beggar appeared with a sack in which he was carrying bread. The children approached him and he gave them some bread and they ate. When he began to leave, they asked him to take them along, but he did not want to. Meanwhile they got a better look at him and realised he was blind, which was very surprising, because if he was blind, how did he find his way? The blind beggar blessed them that they should be like him, saying that they should be old like him. He left them some bread and went on his way.

When the bread was used up, the pair began to cry for food again, when another beggar came. They realised that he was deaf. He also gave them some bread and blessed them that they should be like him. With that, he left them some bread and went on his way. When the bread was used up, they cried out again until another beggar appeared, this time with a speech defect. He also gave them bread, and before he left, blessed them that they should be like him. Later, a beggar with a crooked neck came along, followed by one who was a hunchback, then one without hands, and finally a beggar without feet. Each one gave them bread and blessed them that they should be like him.

When all their bread was used up, the children began walking until they came to an inhabited area. They went from door to door begging, and when they saw that they were successful, they decided to become beggars. Eventually, they became well known to all the beggars. Once, at a major fair in one of the large cities, the beggars got the idea that these two children would be a perfect match for one another. On the king's birthday all the beggars gathered as much meat and bread as possible and made a wedding. The bride and groom were extremely happy, and began remembering the kindness God had shown them when they were in the forest. They wept and yearned for the first beggar — the blind one — who had brought them bread in the forest: "If only he could be here." Suddenly, while they were yearning intensely for the blind beggar, he appeared.

The Story of the Blind Beggar

He spoke up and said:

"Here I am! I've come to be at your wedding. And I'm giving you a wedding present — that you should have a long life like mine. You think I'm blind. Actually I'm not blind at all. But the entire duration of the world's existence is not considered by me to be even so much as the blink of an eye."

This was the reason he appeared blind: he did not look at the world at all. Since the entire duration of the world's existence was not considered by him to be even so much as the blink of an eye, the entire concept of looking at anything in the world or seeing it did not apply to him at all.

"I am extremely old, but I am completely young. I have not yet begun to live, but nevertheless, I am very old. This is not just my own opinion; I also have the word of the Great Eagle. Let me tell you the story.

Once upon a time, people took to the sea in many ships. A great storm came, and shattered the ships. The people, however, survived, and came to a tower. They went up into the tower, and there they found food, drink, clothing, and everything else they needed. All good things, and every pleasure in the world was there.

The people began to converse, and decided that each one should tell an ancient story involving his earliest memory. Each one would tell what he remembered from the time that his memory began. There were old and young people present. They honored the oldest man among them to tell his story first.

'What shall I tell you?' he said. 'I can remember when they cut the apple from the branch.'

No one understood what he meant. However, there were wise men there, and they said, 'This is obviously a very ancient story.'

They then honored the second one to tell his story. The second one, who was not as old as the first, said, 'Is that an old story? I also remember that story! But I can also remember when the lamp was lit.'

'This story is even older than the first!' said the wise men. But they were quite surprised, since the second one was not quite as old as the first, yet he could remember an older event.

They then honored the third one to tell his story. The third one, who was younger than the first two, said, 'I remember when the fruit began to have a structure — that is, when the fruit began to be put together.'

'That story is even older,' they responded.

The fourth one, who was still younger, spoke up: 'I also remember when the seed was brought to plant the fruit.'

The fifth one, who was younger still, said, 'I also remember when the wise men invented the seed.'

The sixth one, who was younger still, said, 'I remember

the taste of the fruit before it entered the fruit.'

The seventh one spoke up and said, 'I remember the fragrance of the fruit before it entered the fruit.'

The eighth one said, 'I remember the appearance of the fruit before it was drawn onto the fruit.'

And I was also there at the time," said the Blind Beggar, "and I was still an infant. I spoke up and said to them, 'I remember all these events, and I remember absolutely nothing.'

'This is a very ancient story,' said the wise men, 'more so than all the others.' They were very surprised that a child remembered more than any of them.

In the midst of this, the Great Eagle came and knocked on the tower. 'Stop being poor! Return to your treasures. make use of your treasures!' He then told them to leave the tower in order of their age, with the oldest going out first.

As he brought them out of the tower, he brought me, the infant, out first, since I was actually older than all the rest, and he was bringing us out in order of age. Actually the youngest was the oldest, and the oldest of them was the youngest.

The Great Eagle then said, 'I will explain the stories that each one told. The first one said he remembered when they cut the apple from the branch. He was saying that he remembered when they cut his umbilical cord. He was saying that he remembered when he was born, and they cut his navel cord.

'The second one said that he remembered when the lamp was burning. He could also remember when he was in his mother's womb, with a lamp burning over his head. The third one said he remembered when the fruit began to form. He could remember when his body began to knit together as the fetus took its form. The fourth one said that he remembered when the seed was brought up to be planted. He remembered how the drop was emitted at the time of conception.

'The fifth one remembered the wise men who discovered the seed. He remembered when the seed was still in the brain. It is the brain's mental power that gives rise to the drop.

The sixth one remembered the taste. This is the *nefesh*- soul. The seventh one remembered the fragrance. This is the *ruach*-spirit. The eighth one remembered the appearance. This is the *neshama*-essence.

'Finally, there was the child who said that he remembered absolutely nothing. He is higher than all the rest, since he remembered even what was before the *nefesh*-soul, the *ruach*-spirit, and the *neshama*-essence. This is the concept of Nothingness.'

The Great Eagle then said to them, 'Return to your ships, which are your bodies. They were shattered, but they will be rebuilt. Now go back to them.' With that, he blessed them.

The Great Eagle then said to me, 'You come with me, since you are just like me. You are very old, and at the same time very young; you have not yet begun to live, but you are extremely old. I am the same, since I am old and at the same time, I am young...'

Therefore, I have the word of the Great Eagle that I have lived a very long life. And now I am giving you my long life as a wedding present."

When the beggar said this, there was tremendous joy and rejoicing there.

*

RABBI NATHAN on TEFILIN

Likutey Halachot, Orach Chayim, Hilchot Tefilin 5

I

Holy Exultation

[1] If you have eyes to see, and you sincerely want to find the truth, the Story of the Seven Beggars will give you a distant glimmer of understanding of the greatness of God and the heights reached by the greatest Tzaddikim of all times. For all the things that the various characters in the story relate about their achievements refer to the spiritual triumphs of one or other of the outstanding Tzaddikim throughout the ages, who exult in the upper worlds about their achievements in this world. Happy are they!

For example, in the portion of the story we are concerned with here, the Story of the Blind Beggar, each of the elders tells his earliest memory. Even the very least of them was on such a high level that it is impossible for us to really understand his true greatness and holiness. Thus the first elder relates that he could remember what happened to him when his umbilical cord was cut. Think about it: is there one person in a whole generation who can genuinely claim to have reached such a level of purity that he could remember what happened to him at the moment of birth, when his umbilical cord was cut? And the elder who remembered this turned out to be the very least of all of them.

From this you can see what a level the second one attained. For him the level of the first was a joke. "That's an old story?" he said. "I remember that story, but I also remember when the light was kindled." This the Great Eagle later interprets to mean that he also remembered what happened to him when he was in his mother's womb, when a lamp shone above his head. Far as we may be from all this, we can still form a faint conception of the superiority of the second elder over the first. For there is a vast difference between a person's state before their entry into this world and after it (see Nidah 30b etc.)

The whole time the embryo is in the womb, a light shines over his head and he is taught the entire Torah, and he sees from one end of the universe to the other. But the moment he emerges into the air of this world, an angel comes and strikes him on the mouth, and he forgets everything. This is what Job meant when he said, "If only I was the way I was in the months of old [i.e. his months in the womb], as at the time when God watched over me, when His lamp shone above my head and by His light I walked through the darkness" (Job 29:2-3, discussed in Nidah loc.cit.)

Man's whole task is to attain the same knowledge and perception he had at first, when the lamp shone over his head and he could see by the hidden light of the Seven Days of Creation and gaze from one end of the universe to the other. Now you can see how far above the level of the first elder the second one was. As far as the heavens are above the earth! The same applies to the third elder as compared with the second, and so with all the others.

Even the least of them was so exalted that only one such Tzaddik appears in the course of several generations. Still, in comparison with the second, he was considered a mere dot. Likewise the second in comparison with the third, and so on — until we come to the one who boasted that he was a complete babe. This is the Blind Beggar himself, who says he remembers all these events and yet he remembers absolute nothingness. It is a fundamental principle in mystical literature that even a very exalted level amounts to no more than a mere dot in relation to the next higher level. Thus the Tikkuney Zohar states: "Even the Supreme Crown is black before the Cause of causes" (Tikkun 70, 123b).

All these amazing wonders are set forth in the Story of the Blind Beggar, told on the first day of the wedding celebration, and many other extraordinary spiritual achievements are discussed in the stories of the other beggars, told on the other days (see Rabbi Nachman's Stories pp. 375-437, and Rabbi Nachman's Tikkun pp. 89-98, where the story of the Sixth Day is discussed). The holy Rebbe Nachman had knowledge of all this, and he knew how to tell each story the way it was, whatever and wherever that may be. When he told this story he said of himself that if he knew nothing at all besides this story he would still be completely unique.

[2] To recapitulate, the story of the First Day describes how they said that each one would tell an old story about his earliest memory. The first elder said he remembered even the cutting of the apple from the branch — i.e. when his umbilical cord was cut. The second elder said he remembered when the lamp was kindled — i.e. when he was in his mother's womb and a lamp shone above his head. The third related that he remembered when the body first began to form. The fourth remembered even when the seed was brought to plant the fruit tree — i.e. the coming of the seed at the time of union.

The fifth could even remember when the sages were inventing the seed — namely when the seed was still in the father's brain. The sixth, seventh and eighth could remember the appearance, the taste and the scent even before they entered the fruit — namely the *nefesh*, *ruach* and *neshamah*. And the baby, the Blind Beggar himself, who related the entire story, said that he could remember absolute nothingness. For he was higher than all of them, and he could remember even what is prior to the *nefesh, ruach* and *neshamah* — that which is called Nothing. If you take an honest, truthful look at this story, you can get a faint glimpse of the wonders of God. Nothing like this has been seen or heard since the world was created.

Expanded Consciousness

The Hebrew term here translated as "expanded consciousness" is mochin d'gadlus. *It is one of the central concepts in this ma'amar. The use of the English expression "expanded consciousness" has no connection with its use in any other religious or meditational traditions, and it should not be confused with popular notions of "altered states of consciousness". The word* mo'ach *refers to the brain, mind or conscious awareness. In Kabbalistic and Chassidic literature, the plural,* mochin, *denotes particular states of knowledge and awareness. The term* mochin d'gadlus, *(sometimes simply* mochin *for short) refers to the enhanced state of awareness of the spiritual plane of existence which is one of the primary goals of the Jewish spiritual seeker and which may be experienced especially at the height of prayer and meditation.*

Mochin d'gadlus is particularly associated with Da'at, *knowledge, because the state of mind in question involves a knowledge and understanding of the array of the Ten Sefirot: these are the Divine attributes which lie behind the visible Creation and through which the Creation flows forth from its hidden Source. Thus* mochin d'gadlus *is a higher level than simple* Emunah, *faith, which one can have even without knowledge. A person may have a strong belief in God and His presence without a refined* knowledge *of His ways and how He relates to the Creation.* Emunah, *the belief in God, is however the necessary gateway to* mochin d'gadlus.

As will become amply clear in the course of Rabbi Nathan's ma'mar, mochin d'gadlus *is not an absolute state that is achieved once and for all. The religious seeker starts off with simple* Emunah. *Then, through intense prayer, study, contemplation and further prayer, he may be graced with expanded consciousness, but only for a time. It is the nature of our limited minds that after a while the expanded consciousness leaves us, and we return to* mochin d'katnus, *restricted consciousness.*

Each prayer, then, is an opportunity to reach out for new levels and dimensions of knowledge and understanding of God. These in turn enhance the Emunah *which stays with one even after the intensity of the prayer-experience has passed. This deepened* Emunah *then inspires one to search for greater knowledge and understanding.*

[3] The whole story of the Blind Beggar is connected with the Tefilin. One of the key ideas of the Tefilin is memory: they are to be "for *memory* between your eyes" (Exodus 13:9). Why "between your eyes"? Because the kind of memory we have depends on what we do with our eyes. This is clear from the story. The beggar who tells it was "completely blind" — i.e. he did not look at this material world at all. He had reached a level where the entire world did not amount to the blink of an eye as far as he was concerned. In this sense he had achieved perfect vision, and this was what enabled him to develop his memory to the ultimate level of perfection, so that he could remember more than all the others. Memory depends upon the eyes. (See also Likutey Moharan I:54).

The Tefilin involve more than simply the physical objects — the parchment and leather Torah portions, capsules and straps

— with which the mitzva is performed. Tefilin is a spiritual concept — a concept of expanded consciousness. Expanded consciousness is a state of enhanced spiritual awareness and knowledge in which one reaches a deeper understanding of Godliness than when involved in one's mundane affairs. This expanded consciousness is what is here called memory — memory in its holy aspect (see Likutey Moharan I:37, where the concept of "memory" is equated with understanding and expanded consciousness).

The Tefilin contain Torah passages — the *parshiyot*: spiritual Torah written on physical parchment. There are four *parshiyot* in the Tefilin of the Head, the *shel rosh*, and four in the Tefilin of the Arm, the *shel yad*. These eight passages correspond to the eight holy elders in the story, who were masters of memory. For the Tefilin are "for *memory* between your eyes".

The *Tefilin shel rosh*, the Head Tefilin, is associated with the male (influencing) aspect of Godliness, while the *Tefilin shel yad*, the Arm Tefilin, is associated with the female (receptive) aspect. The two together are associated with the state of expanded consciousness known as "gestation" (P'ri Etz Chayim, Sha'ar HaTefilin, Ch.1). See below # 29-32 for fuller discussion of the idea of pregnancy and birth.) Similarly, these eight holy elders, who achieved such exalted levels of consciousness that each one could remember way back, are divided into two groups of four, corresponding to the two sets of four parshiyot in the *shel yad* and the *shel rosh*.

Thus when the first four elders told their stories, all their memories related to their experiences *after* entry into the womb. One boasted that he could remember when they brought the seed to plant the fruit tree — the entry of the drop of seed. The second remembered the formation of the fruit, the third how the lamp was alight — namely the whole period of pregnancy. The fourth and last remembered the moment of completion of the new baby as an independent being — the cutting of the umbilical cord, marking his first entry into this world. Everything they remembered is bound up with God's miracles with the child while inside and attached to the mother, and thus their levels of consciousness are "female". They thus correspond to the four *parshiyot* of the *shel yad*, which, as we saw above, are associated with the "female aspect" and the corresponding levels of consciousness.

The second group of four elders, on the other hand, could remember even further back, *before* the seed came into the mother's womb. They could remember when the seed was still in the brain of the father: they could recall the appearance, the taste and the scent — the *nefesh, ruach* and *neshamah*. The thought originates in a most exalted place, and comes down from level to level, from cause to effect, from world to world, through the levels of *nefesh, ruach* and *neshamah* — until there comes about the thought through which the holy drop from which the child will be formed comes into being. These four stages all take place in the father, the male. This is why the elders who could remember these stages correspond to the *parshiyot* of the *shel rosh*, which are associated with the "male consciousness" and the corresponding levels of consciousness.

The spiritual roots of the mitzva of Tefilin lie in the Godly aspect known as the Holy Beard. [Since Man was created in the image of God, the various parts of the human form correspond to different aspects of the Divine revelation in the Creation. God's inner intention in bringing about the Creation as a whole is too exalted to be revealed within the Creation, and is alluded to by the brain, which is likewise not visible: it is concealed within the skull. Via the skull, the brain gives vitality to all the many hairs of the beard. Now the beard *is* visible to the onlooker, and thus the hairs of the beard signify how the many details of the created worlds derive from a single unifying Divine intention.]

The Holy Beard is the source of long life. The Hebrew

word for beard, ZaKaN, is made up of the same letters as the word for an old man or elder — ZaKeN. The eight elders in the story — corresponding to the eight *parshiyot* of the Tefilin — all embody different aspects of the Holy Beard. And all these eight elders receive from the Supreme Elder, the greatest of them all, who was also the youngest of them all — the Blind Beggar, who was a complete baby. He is the very source of long life and old age. All the eight holy elders — the eight *parshiyot* of the Tefilin — derive from him. However his level of consciousness is so exalted that it cannot even be clothed in any of the *parshiyot* of the Tefilin. This is why there is no *parashah* corresponding to him.

For he is more exalted than all of them: he is their root. He is the source of all the states of expanded consciousness associated with the Tefilin, as embodied in the eight holy elders. For he himself is merged in the Infinite. This is why his state of consciousness is not called memory at all. The Tefilin express the idea of memory, but this Supreme Elder's state of consciousness goes *beyond* memory, as he himself says when he tells us he remembers all this and yet he remembers nothing. In other words he could remember everything the others remembered, because he encompasses them all, and all of them receive their consciousness and memory from him. Yet his own consciousness cannot itself be called memory: it is *beyond* memory and its very source, because he is absorbed in the Infinite. This is why he has no corresponding *parashah*, because he is more exalted than all of the elders and all the *parshiyot* — he is their source.

Life

[4] The states of expanded consciousness associated with the Tefilin can be summed up in one word: life! The Rabbis thus taught that those who put on Tefilin attain life. "God is upon them..." (i.e. the name of God, which is written inside the

Tefilin and is also formed through the knots and the way the Tefilin are bound.) "...they will *live*" (Isaiah 38:16 discussed in Menachot 44b.) The mitzva of Tefilin gives us life and vitality, because wisdom, spiritual perception and expanded consciousness *are* life. "Wisdom gives life to those who possess it." (Ecclesiastes 7:12)

The Tefilin are associated with the three divine names EKYEH, YKVK, EKYEH, the numerical value of whose letters is the same as that of the letters of HaYYiM, life — the life of the spirit. (P'ri Etz Chayim, Sha'ar HaTefilin, Ch.1. Wherever the Hebrew letter *Heh* appears in a Divine Name, it is transliterated here with a K, as the Divine Name should not be pronounced the way it is written, nor should it be destroyed even when printed in English.)

For the states of consciousness associated with the Tefilin derive from the Holy Beard — comprising all the holy elders in the story, all of whom are rooted in the Supreme Elder, the Blind Beggar, who boasted that his was the truly long life, because he was very old... yet he was still a suckling babe and he hadn't even begun to live... yet he was very old and all the time of the world did not amount to so much as the blink of an eye as far as he was concerned.

All these matters involve the hidden secrets of the Ancient of Days, which are beyond the grasp of thought, and no-one on earth can find the interpretation or tell the secret. Even so, the Rebbe did tell the story, and his words have been put down in writing and printed — all through God's love for His people. So it is only fitting that we should search for some hints we can apply in our own practical lives in order to wake up from our spiritual sleep. This was the Rebbe's whole purpose in telling his stories — to awaken all the people who are sleeping away their lives. (See Likutey Moharan I:60,6).

[5] As far as practical day to day life is concerned, the key idea is something I saw at first hand in the Rebbe's own

life over and over again. He was always living a new life. Several times I heard him say, "The life I had today was like nothing I've ever had before." Other times he commented that people use the word "life" to refer to all different kinds of life. Life may be painful, and there are many different kinds of pain. All the different kinds of life are called life (see Tzaddik #8; #400). But the only real life in the true sense of the word is the long life lived by the Blind Beggar. He boasted that he was very old... and yet he was very young... and he hadn't even begun to live yet!

Life in the true sense of the word is when we constantly make a new start with our spiritual work as if we had not even begun yet. The Shema says: "...these words that I am commanding you *today* should be on your heart" (Deuteronomy 6:6). *Today* — because "each day you should see them as totally new. Don't look at them as an old set of ordinances which no-one cares about. Each day they should be *new*" (Sifri ad loc.) Similarly, "Pay attention and listen, Israel: *today* you have become God's people" (Deuteronomy 27:9) — "Each day you should think of it as if you have just entered the covenant with God today." (See Rashi ad loc.)

I saw this with the Rebbe over and over again. One moment he would reach amazing spiritual heights and reveal extraordinary teachings the like of which had never been heard. Then immediately afterwards we would see him miserable and dejected. Sometimes he would tell us why, pouring out his heart in sorrow, asking how one succeeds at being a good Jew. He would speak like someone who had never had the slightest taste of spiritual life. To describe this to somebody who never actually saw it is virtually impossible. The Rebbe was constantly saying, "Now I know nothing, absolutely nothing!" — even though just a moment before he had revealed the most powerful teachings and attained outstanding heights of spirituality. Only a moment later he would be saying that now he knew nothing at all.

Quite simply, the Rebbe never stood still for a moment. He never stayed on the same level. He was always moving forward as fast as he could from one level to the next, ever forwards, until he reached the most exalted heights. And even when he achieved them, he was still not satisfied.

Making a Start

The secret of life is to constantly make a new start with one's spiritual work. Spiritual work, the service of God, *is* life — "for this [the Torah] *is your life*" (Deuteronomy 30:20). The whole key to spiritual life is *starting* — constantly making a new start, applying oneself with ever renewed efforts, and never allowing oneself to fall into old age in the unholy sense. Never let your prayer and other devotions become stale and routine. This is what the Rebbe meant when he said it is no good to be old (Rabbi Nachman's Wisdom #51). An old Tzaddik is no good and an old Chassid is no good! Being old is no good at all! We should always start all over again — all the time!

This was the key to the long life of the Blind Beggar. He was old and young at the same time. The older he got and the more he became merged with the Ancient One, the younger he became — because each time he had a deeper perception of how far he was from God, whose "greatness is unsearchable" (Psalms 145:3). The more he became merged with the holy, the more he understood that he had not *begun* to live at all. In the end he attained long life in the true sense of the term — a life in which youthfulness and old age come together in a way that is ultimately beyond comprehension.

This whole idea is expressed in the mitzva of Tefilin, which derives from this holy elder — for as we have seen, he is the root of the Tefilin and of the states of expanded consciousness they are associated with. Of the Tefilin, the Torah says: "You who are *attached* to HaShem your God are all *alive* today"

(Deuteronomy 4:4). The main idea of the Tefilin is to live new life at all times — to renew one's life like the eagle and constantly make a new start with one's spiritual work, never falling into the kind of unholy old age which makes everything seem stale and routine. Everything should always be completely new and fresh, as if you haven't even begun yet. This applies even to the greatest Tzaddik, who may have devoted years of work and effort to his devotions. When you consider how the entire Creation is constantly renewed day after day, even such a Tzaddik hasn't begun!

For God is always doing new things. "In His goodness He renews the creation constantly, every day." (From the blessing before the morning Shema). No day is like any other. Every day and every moment, God works new wonders. No one day is ever like the next, and no one moment is like any other. From moment to moment the worlds are in a constant state of flux and change. The variety is infinite, awesome and full of wonder.

What is most amazing of all is that the vital flow coming into the worlds depends entirely on the efforts of man in this world. Everything depends upon us, from beginning to end. And this is why we have to constantly make fresh efforts in our work for God, according to the ever-changing needs of all the worlds and the needs of the creative process at each particular moment. For every fresh moment brings with it a new revelation of Godliness. "Day speaks to day, and night reveals knowledge to night" (Psalms 19:3). Every day, every night, every minute and every second, God's greatness is revealed in a completely new way unparalleled in all the creation.

This is why you have to start afresh each time. Every day, look at the Torah and the mitzvot as completely new. This is the key to long life and vitality. As the Rebbe put it: with each passing day you should make the day longer by adding more holiness, and more knowledge and wisdom (see

Likutey Moharan 60:3). Each day always starts off being very short, in the sense that there seems to be so much to do. Everything seems such a burden. We have to see to it to extend the day — to lengthen it by adding new holiness and purity. This is the key to long life — to start afresh each time, putting in new efforts and extra determination. No matter what we may have achieved in the past, we should forget about it completely. The important thing is *now*. We have to make a completely new start.

We achieve this through the Tefilin. The essential idea of putting on Tefilin day by day is to achieve *life* — for "You who are bound to Hashem your God are all *alive* today". The idea of constant renewal is the central element in the state of vitality and expanded consciousness deriving from the Supreme Elder who is the source of the Tefilin. He had long life because he combined old age and youth together — as taught in the Psalms (103:5): "Renew your youth like the eagle". "The older this eagle becomes," the Rabbis commented, "the more youthful it becomes" (see Rashi ad loc.) In other words, the older it becomes, the more it renews its life, making a fresh start each time. It is always only just beginning to live. This is why in the story, the Blind Beggar had the agreement of the Great Eagle. And this constant renewal is the underlying idea of the Tefilin and the key to life.

Patience

[6] The essential idea of the Tefilin, then, is that a higher state of mind should shine within us. We have seen that this inner light derives from the Holy Beard. The Light of the Holy Beard, also called the Light of the Face, is expressed in the Thirteen Attributes of God's Lovingkindness (Exodus 34:6-7). The root of all of them is the victory over anger. Out of love, God sets aside the stern way of dealing with the world that strict justice demands. Instead, He sweetens the

judgement. This quality is called "slow to anger" — namely, patience.

Patience is the root of all the other Thirteen Attributes, as we learn from a comment the Rabbis made on the passage describing the revelation of the Thirteen Attributes to Moses. At the moment of the revelation, the Torah tells us that "Moses hurried and bowed his head towards the earth" (Exodus 34:8). "What did he see that made him do this?" asked the Rabbis. And they replied: "He saw *patience*!" (Sanhedrin 111a.) Patience — the victory over anger — is the key to all the other attributes. This was why Moses was so moved when it was revealed to him.

Patience is one of the most important qualities every Jew needs (see Likutey Moharan I:155). It is a basic principle that a Jew should try to model himself on the Creator and cultivate the Thirteen Attributes of Lovingkindness in himself. Patience means not to let anything make you angry or upset. Pay no attention to all the obstacles and distractions you encounter as you go about your search for spiritual advance.

There are many different kinds of obstacles. Some come from the world around us. Other people may put all kinds of barriers in your way. Even the people closest to you — parents or parents-in-law, your wife, husband or other relatives and friends — may do so. Everyone has experience of this. As soon as someone starts trying to follow a spiritual path and begins making efforts to pray with concentration and so on, he or she is immediately confronted with an endless succession of obstacles from the people around them. The only way to fight is with determination: you have to be "bold as a leopard and strong as a lion" (Avot 5:24) to do God's will and overcome all the obstacles. You must do your part. Carry on with your prayers and studies etc. as best as you can and try not to pay any attention at all to the distractions. This is what is meant by patience: don't allow yourself to get impatient or frustrated. Don't stop trying just because of the obstacles.

Keep going, be patient, and pay no attention at all.

The same applies to the various distractions which come from within ourselves — our material desires, the various negative thoughts and feelings we have, and so on. You may feel hounded by them constantly, and especially when you are trying to pray. This may cause you a lot of anguish. Still, you must be patient. Patience is an aspect of faith: the belief that everything is sent by God. Strengthen yourself in your faith in God and in the power of the Tzaddikim and their teachings. Work on your determination and press on with your efforts. Don't let anything trouble you or pull you down. Do you have a nagging voice inside you putting all kinds of confusing thoughts into your mind, and telling you that everything is futile and hopeless, especially after all the wrong you have done in your life and all your past failures? Just pay no attention.

There is no such thing as no hope in this world — despair does not exist! Even if you have failed time and time again, that is no reason to give up. Press on determinedly and start all over again — every day of your life. Don't get old in the unholy sense. Getting the idea that we have grown old in our sins is the root cause of all our failures and discouragement. People slip into thinking they are so habituated to their bad ways, there is no hope at all of their ever getting out of them. This is not true. We have to believe and know that every single day and every moment, each individual has the power to become a completely new person.

Renewal

God is constantly creating. No one day or moment is like any other. That is why you must always press on and start all over again. Sometimes you may have to make a new start several times all in the same day (see Rabbi Nachman's Wisdom #48). You may feel you are making no progress at all. Even so, always try to remember God's creative power, the power of innovation and renewal, and just forget about whatever may have happened in the past. Start now! Don't allow yourself to get disheartened.

This is what is meant by patience: to take a deep breath, letting all the obstacles and distractions pass over you without paying attention to any of them, not getting upset, not flinching and not losing heart in any way. Take strength from God as much as you can. God is constantly full of love. His kindness is unending, His love is inexhaustible.

It is well worth repeating these basic ideas over and over again, because they are the key to all success in life. The whole reason why people are so far from God is because they have become discouraged. It is nothing less than tragic — because by allowing their efforts to flag and fall away to nothing, they are losing all the good of the World to Come they could otherwise have. Some people try once to serve God, but as soon as they are put to the test they fall down and then get so discouraged that they give up. Others make a second effort and try again once or twice. But when they see how they just keep on falling down, they too loose heart and feel they simply don't have the strength to start again any more. All this is the work of the Evil One. The Evil One is called the Old Man of the Sitra Achra, the Other Side. (The Other Side is the realm of everything that is unholy.) This is the "old and foolish king" of Kohelet (Ecclesiastes 4:13). He tries his best to make us feel old and weak by putting it into our minds that we are so far gone in our bad ways, we will never be able to change.

It simply is not true. Every day each person wakes up a completely new being — which is why we recite all the morning blessings every day, because each day we become a new person (see Tur, Orach Chayim 46 and Taz on Orach Chayim 4:1). "He gives strength to the weary" (Morning Blessings) is a blessing over the renewal of our mental and spiritual powers and vitality.

Take good care not to slip into unholy old age. Keep strong and renew yourself every moment. Each day and every moment you should feel as if you were born *today*! As if you received the Torah *today*! "Each day you should look on the Torah and the mitzvot as if they are new". Pay no attention to obstacles and barriers. This is what being patient means.

The Holy Elder in the story is the perfect example of this patience. He is the true elder, because he really has a long life in the true sense of the term. He is always starting afresh, and this is the key to long life. When a person feels their spiritual work is old and stale, or worse still, if they feel they have grown old in their bad ways, this is not old age at all, but the opposite. This way of living makes the time very short. People who are not constantly developing and growing in holiness are called "short-lived and full of anger" (see Likutey Moharan II:4).

The Righteous, the Wicked, and those in between

[7] Anyone who cares about their ultimate destiny must be very careful not to be old at all — i.e. not to fall into the old-age mentality of the Other Side. This applies to everyone, from the greatest Tzaddikim to the medium individual and even the lowest of the low: everyone must take good care never to fall into this kind of old-old mentality.

Even a great Tzaddik must not allow himself to get old in his devotions, even if he has already attained very high levels. He still has to carry on climbing from level to level. Each time he must start all over again. This is the essence of Judaism: to push on determinedly, constantly climbing from level to level. I heard this directly from the Rebbe as he began his teaching on "The Nine Precious Perfections of the Beard" (Likutey Moharan I:20). His precise words were,

"Someone who wants to be an Israelite, *namely to go from level to level*, can only do so by means of Eretz Yisrael, the Land of Israel." The implication is that a Jew is defined as someone who is always moving from level to level. This is the only real long life — when a person constantly starts afresh.

At the other end of the spectrum, even a person who has done much wrong must still not be old. Such a person needs to be particularly wary not to fall into the old-age mentality, in order not to fall into despair. The nagging voice inside says, "You're already such an old sinner, you'll never be able to change." Someone with a long history of wrong-doing needs to make a determined effort to make a new start. The all important thing is to do *something* holy, big or small! Even if the only thing you can do is to say one word of prayer or study the tiniest amount, you should do whatever you can and take heart from the share you do have in the holiness of the Jewish People.

For no matter how low you may feel yourself to be, you certainly do many mitzvot every day, because "even the Jewish sinners are full of mitzvot like a pomegranate" (Eruvin 19a). You have to look for your good points and constantly take heart from them, as explained in Rebbe Nachman's teaching of *Azamra* (Breslov Research Institute 1984). Never give up! Start over every time, so that you won't loose everything. Whatever you can do, do with all your strength. The main thing is patience: you need to be infinitely patient. Take a long breath and never loose hope of God's help. Pay no attention to the obstacles and distractions.

[8] This explains a comment of the Rabbis on God's attribute of patience (Exodus 34:6). The Hebrew term for it, *erech apayim*, is a plural form, suggesting at least two kinds of patience. Thus the Rabbis said, God shows "patience to the righteous and patience to the wicked" (Baba Kama 50a).

Why do the righteous, the Tzaddikim need this quality of

patience? Because for them the threat of the old-old mentality of the Other Side is that of getting into a groove with their devotions. They must constantly renew themselves and make a new start every day, adding extra holiness without ever tiring. They must let nothing distract them and push them off their path. Sometimes people who serve God get tired because of all the suffering they have gone through, and this can push them into weakness and old age. This is why the Tzaddikim need the quality of patience every day of their lives, in order to bear up to the weight of the efforts involved and constantly start afresh.

On the other hand God shows "patience to the wicked" in the sense that he leaves them alone all their lives in the hope that one day they will repent. "Until the day of his death You await him in case he will repent" (Yom Kippur liturgy). Since the wicked are given this chance to repent, they too need this quality of patience in order that their own evil should not prevent them from coming back to God. A person who has done wrong should never allow him- or herself to become discouraged by the thought of all their sins, or by the fact that they may have tried to change themselves in the past only to fall away time after time. They must still trust in God's great kindness, patiently bearing everything they may have to go through. They need to make strong efforts to start afresh at all times and never think of themselves as old and hardened sinners. Maybe this time they *will* be able to take themselves in hand and leave their old thoughts and ways behind.

This constant renewal is the key to *teshuvah*, the return to God. So everyone — the Tzaddikim, the sinners, and certainly all the people who come somewhere in between — need to develop this quality of patience.

Attachment to the Tzaddik

[9] The strength to win through comes from the Blind Beggar — the holy elder who is the Elder of the Elders, who attained such a level of old age in the holy sense that he could say of himself "I am very old, but I am very young". He is the one from whom the Tzaddikim themselves get the strength they need in order to persist in their devotions and constantly renew their efforts. Then, even when they reach the highest levels, which only the truly outstanding masters attain, they still do not content themselves with their achievements. They say, "Who knows, there may be more!" — and start all over again. This is how they constantly reach new and amazing levels of perception.

And it is the strength of these Tzaddikim which gives courage even to the people lower down, who find themselves constantly falling, and helps them start again each time. In our present dark exile the forces of evil attack everyone who wants to try to serve God. They find themselves thrown down again and again, each in their own way. People need constant encouragement in order not to just give up and loose hope completely. It is only from the Tzaddikim that they can get the strength to carry on, because the more sick the patient, the greater the doctor he needs (see Likutey Moharan I:30). Because of their unremitting efforts, these Tzaddikim reach such ever-heightened levels of perception of God's supreme lovingkindness that they are able to understand how God is constantly devising means of helping even the lowest of the low to make sure no-one will be thrown away.

It is their perception of God's love that gives these Tzaddikim the ability to inspire and encourage even those who have fallen very low. They teach them not to let anything push them down but to carry on determinedly, bearing everything, in the faith that God's Lovingkindness is never exhausted and that they should press on, constantly making new efforts to come closer to God to the best of their ability.

These great Tzaddikim are constantly starting all over again. Even when they reach the most exalted levels — levels many other outstanding Tzaddikim never reached, levels so high they seem as though they must be the ultimate level — they still do not content themselves with what they have achieved so far. Instead they begin thinking out ways of starting all over again and striving even higher, even when they don't have the faintest notion of what might be beyond. They say, "Who knows what there might be!"

I heard this from the Rebbe himself. Once he was pouring out his heart to me, saying "How can one succeed at being a Jew?" To me this was amazing, because only a little while earlier he had revealed the most exalted Torah. The Rebbe said to me, "Who knows what more there might be to attain. When I started out it never occurred to me to even think of striving for the perceptions I have reached so far. In that case who knows what still lies ahead of me?" This was always his way throughout his life. (Rabbi Nachman's Wisdom #159.)

The great Tzaddikim reason that God is infinite and therefore it must be possible that there is more to achieve in this world. And so they start all over again — and this is how they actually rise up to an even higher level. Then they say, "Who knows, there might be even more!" and they start all over again.

Tzaddikim like these give strength to all the people who keep on falling down, proving that there is no such thing as no hope in this world. There is no despair and no giving up! Sometimes a person falls so low, he thinks he will never get up this time. But who knows God's greatness and lovingkindness? God's love is so great that there must be a way of getting up even from there! Even if a person falls down over and over again, God forbid, every little effort he makes to lift himself up, every cry, even from the lowest depths of hell, is very dear to God. Nothing is ever lost.

God is infinite and His Torah is infinite. Compared with the greatness of God, even the greatest heights in the world are nothing. And so too, for every fall in the world, there is always something worse. Since things could always be worse, one must fight hard not to fall further. The strength to do so comes from these great Tzaddikim who never stand still but constantly climb higher. Just as there is no real ascent in the world, so there is no fall that you cannot get up from. The higher the Tzaddik rises, the more he understands God's lovingkindness — this is the essence of God's greatness.

In Torah literature the attribute of lovingkindness is in fact termed "greatness", as the commentaries explain on the verse, "For yours, Hashem, is the greatness" (Chronicles I, 29:11). So the more one understands God's greatness, the more one understands His unending lovingkindness and compassion. Thus it is the Tzaddikim who are constantly rising higher and higher that come to understand that there is no fall in the world and no despair — because they grasp that there is a level of Divine lovingkindness that extends even to those who have fallen to the lowest depths.

This explains Rebbe Nachman's comment in his teaching in Likutey Moharan I:30 that one needs to search out the greatest Tzaddik, because the more sick the patient the greater the doctor he needs. The greater the Tzaddik, the greater his power to lift up even those who have fallen the lowest. Through the strength of the Tzaddikim there is no fall in the world you cannot get up from if you will just have faith and draw close to them.

So the Tzaddikim on their level need patience in order to continue pushing forward without becoming complacent because of their great achievements so far. They must constantly look ahead and strive to come to even greater levels. And those who are low down, on the other hand, even those who have fallen into the worst extremes of evil, as long as they still have the breath of life in them, as long as they can still move a single limb... they too must be patient. They must constantly wait and hope for God's help, and make whatever efforts they can to start all over again. They must know that nothing is ever lost: not a single gesture or a sigh or a cry, not even a throb of desire in the heart. For "God will not despise for ever" (Lamentations 3:31).

II

The *Ma'barta* and the *Retzu'ot*

[10] All of the ideas explained above are expressed in the Tefilin. It is through the mitzva of Tefilin that we draw down the expanded consciousness and vitality we have been discussing from the holy elders, who in turn receive it from the Supreme Elder, the Blind Beggar.

[11] The *ma'barta* (literally the crossing or ford) is the part of each *bayit*, the capsule, where the *retzu'a*, the strap, passes through. The underlying idea of the *Ma'ABaRta* is related to the idea of the "ford of Yabok" (*Ma'AVaR Yabok* — Genesis 32:23) which Jacob had to cross on his way back from Laban's house to the Land of Israel (P'ri Etz Chayim, Sha'ar HaTefilin, Ch.1). Let us understand why.

We have discussed how the expanded consciousness which comes through the Tefilin is drawn from the Light of the Face — revealed in the Thirteen Attributes of Lovingkindness, all of which are included in the quality of patience (above #3 and #6). The light is drawn down to us by the straps, the *retzu'ot*, by which we attach the Tefilin to the head and the arm. Because of this the numerical value of the Hebrew letters of the word ReTZU'AH is 370, corresponding to the three hundred and seventy radiations of the Light of the Face [These three hundred and seventy radiations correspond to the Ten Sefirot. The upper three — Wisdom, Understanding and Knowledge — are each counted as hundreds — hence 300; the lower seven — from Chessed to Malchut — are each counted as tens and therefore equal 70, giving a total of 370. Sha'ar HaKavanot, Tefilin, D'rush 2.]

The straps are long, alluding to the quality of *long*-suffering and patience. This is the quality that helps us overcome the "evil strap" — this is the punitive whip of suffering which is used to beat sinners. This "evil strap" is the source of all the severe judgements and suffering in the world. Through the long straps of the *retzu'ot*, which connect with the Light of the Face, we draw down on ourselves the quality of patience — the expanded consciousness associated with the Tefilin. This helps us to overcome all the hardship and difficulties we may have to go through in life, sweetening the pain, so that nothing can interfere with our efforts to come closer to God.

Patience means taking a deep, long breath no matter what we may have to confront, keeping cool even when faced with pain, hardship and obstacles. We have to do our part: instead of letting our difficulties push us off course, we have to carry on with our work of Torah and devotion as best as we can until eventually we overcome all our problems. If we refuse to take our difficulties to heart, they will eventually automatically loose their power to trouble us. This is because the only reason why suffering and obstacles are sent to us in the first place is to test us. If we remain firm, take a long deep breath, and pay no attention to them, we overcome the test! This is why the long *retzu'ot* nullify the power of the evil strap which is the source of all suffering in the world, making everything sweeter.

The reason why the *ma'barta* is associated with the concept of the *ma'avar Yabok*, the "ford of Yabok", is that the letters of YaBoK have the same numerical value (112) as that of the letters of the two names of God, YKVK (26) and ELOKIM (86). The name YKVK alludes to the attribute of God's lovingkindness, while ELOKIM alludes to God's attribute of strict justice. King David brought the two sides together in a unity when he said, "In YKVK I will give praise for the matter, in ELOKIM I will give praise for the matter" (Psalms 56:11).

We have to praise and acknowledge God and draw close to Him at all times, whether we go up or down — whether things are good, flowing from the attribute of lovingkindness, or seemingly bad, flowing from the attribute of strict justice. (See Likutey Moharan I:33).

We have to be skillful (Hebrew = BoKY) in our spiritual journey. The skill we need is to be able to bring the two sides together. Rebbe Nachman thus teaches that anyone who wants to return to God has to be skillful at all stages in the spiritual journey — whether they go up or fall down. The skill is to find God in all situations. "If I go up to Heaven, You are there; and if I make my bed in Hell, behold, You are there" (Psalms 139:8). We have to see to it that we are getting closer to God at all times and in all places, whether we feel we have made advances or have fallen down. Even someone who has fallen to the lowest depths of hell can still draw close to God (Likutey Moharan I:6).

The underlying idea here is exactly the same as the patience and long-suffering we have been discussing — taking a long breath at all times, regardless of the situation we find ourselves in, allowing nothing in the world to push us down, constantly starting again in our efforts to come close to God without flagging. Even if you rise to very great heights, you must still know that God is in Heaven. Sometimes you may think you have risen so high that you *are* in Heaven. But you still have to start all over again and search for God, because it is dangerously easy to become complacent.

All these ideas are alluded to in the *ma'barta* and the associated idea of the *ma'avar Yabok*, the "ford of Yabok". The letters of YaBoK are exactly the same as the letters making up the word for skillful, BaKY (see Likutey Moharan I:6 end). In addition, the letters of YaBoK have the same numerical value as the letters of the two names of God YKVK and ELOKIM, as we have seen. In bringing the two names together we have the idea expressed in the verse "In YKVK I will give praise for the matter, in ELOKIM I will give praise for the matter" (Psalms 56:11) — that we should acknowledge God and try to draw closer at all times, whether we experience His quality of lovingkindness or that of strict justice, whether we go up or down. In serving God we must be patient and persistent at all times, letting nothing push us down or distract us, never tiring or losing our enthusiasm.

The word *ma'barta* literally means the crossing point: by means of the long *retzu'ot* of the Tefilin, which pass through the *ma'barta*, we pass over and conquer all the suffering, the obstacles and the distractions which come from the evil strap. Nothing can stand in the way of this patience.

When God revealed His Thirteen Attributes of Lovingkindness to Moses, it is written that "God *passed by* in front of him" (Exodus 34:6). This concept of passing by is the concept of the *ma'barta*, signifying a crossing. For when God passed by, He revealed to Moses the Thirteen Attributes of Lovingkindness. It was then that "Moses made haste and bowed his head toward the earth" (ibid v.8). As mentioned earlier, the Rabbis commented that Moses then grasped the quality of patience — the concept of the Tefilin — through which we overcome everything so as to be able to draw close to God. Here again we have the idea of the *ma'barta* — God "*passed by*".

In the same passage it is written: "I will make all My goodness pass before you..." (ibid. v.19) "...and you will see My back" (v.23) The Rabbis stated that the "back" alludes to the knot, the *kesher*, in the *retzu'ot* of the Head Tefilin (Berachot 7), because it is in the Thirteen Attributes of God's Lovingkindness, which were then revealed, that the Tefilin are rooted.

The *Parshiyot* — Faith

[12] The way to come to patience is through faith, *Emunah*. Faith is same idea as Eretz Yisrael, the Land of Israel (See

Likutey Moharan I:155). All of the four *parshiyot* of the Tefilin, the parchment slips inscribed with Torah passages, are concerned with the ideas of faith and Eretz Yisrael. Thus the main theme of the first two *parshiyot* (Exodus 13:1-10 and ibid. 11-16) is the Exodus from Egypt and the entry into the Land of Israel. The first *par'shah* says, "Remember this day that you came out of Egypt..." (Exodus 13:3) and "It shall be when God will bring you to the land..." (ibid. 5). And the first words of the second *par'shah* are: "And it shall be when God will bring you into the land..." (ibid. 11).

This is because the quality of patience, which is the essential idea of the Tefilin, is achieved through Eretz Yisrael, which is the opposite of Egypt. Egypt was full of idolatrous cults — the denial of faith. That was why, when the Children of Israel were in exile in Egypt, "they did not listen to Moses because of *impatience* of spirit" (Exodus 6:9). They could not come close to the Tzaddik — Moses — because of their impatience, the opposite of the patience and long-suffering we need to come close to God and the Tzaddikim.

The way to come to patience is through faith, and this is the subject of the last two *parshiyot* of the Tefilin, which are the first and second paragraphs of the Shema (Deuteronomy 6:4-9 and 11:13-21). The Shema is the declaration of our faith in the unity of God. The second paragraph, "And it shall be if you will listen", also speaks about taking on the yoke of the mitzvot and the rejection of idolatry. Idolatry is associated with "hot anger", the opposite of patience. Thus it is written there, "Take care of yourselves, lest you turn aside and serve other gods, and the *anger of God will wax hot...*" (Deuteronomy 11, 16-17).

The whole purpose of the Exodus from Egypt — the place of idolatry and anger — was to bring the Children of Israel to the Land of Israel — the place of faith and patience. And thus we see that all four *parshiyot* of the Tefilin are concerned with faith and patience — the essential themes of the Tefilin.

This is why the conclusion of the last *par'shah* speaks about long life: "in order that your days may be multiplied, and the days of your children..." (ibid. v.21). The patience we come to through the Tefilin brings us to long life, because the basis of all life is the breath — the long breath of patience, as discussed earlier. And thus the Rabbis said: "The life of angry people is no life at all" (Pesachim 113). Someone who is angry is the opposite of patient, and since patience is the basis of long life, the angry person has no life.

[13] The reason for binding the Arm Tefilin on the *left* arm is because the left arm is the weak arm, the source of all suffering and obstacles. The purpose of the Tefilin is to counter them all with patience and thereby conquer everything.

The Sanctity of the First-Born

[15] The first *par'shah* of the Tefilin opens with the commandment to sanctify the first-born: "And God spoke to Moses saying: Sanctify unto Me all the first-born, whatever opens the womb among the Children of Israel..." (Exodus 13: 2).

The whole idea of the Tefilin is intimately bound up with the sanctity of the first-born, which in turn is associated with the Exodus from Egypt. The Exodus itself was in fact a birth — the birth of the whole Jewish People, the first-born. It is because of the Exodus that we are commanded to sanctify the first-born — as we find in the second *par'shah*: "And it came to pass when Pharaoh refused to let us go that God slew all the first-born in the land of Egypt... therefore I sacrifice to God all that opens the womb..." (ibid. 15). All this is in order to bring about the birth of the expanded consciousness within us — this is the real birth: to constantly renew our vital energy and spiritual powers as if we had just been born today. This is the essence of long life, the underlying idea of the Tefilin.

The reason why the first-born is given to the priest or redeemed from him is because the priest represents the Holy Elder. Thus the Psalms speak of "precious oil upon the head, coming down upon the beard, even Aaron's beard..." (Psalms 133:2). Aaron was the high-priest. His beard (Heb.= *ZaKaN*) alludes to the Holy Elder (Heb.= *ZaKeN*). (As regards the oil, it is written: "Let not oil be lacking from your head" (Ecclesiastes 9:8). On this the Rabbis commented, "this refers to the Head Tefilin" (Shabbos 151). This is because the inner light of the Tefilin is drawn from the "precious oil on the head, coming down upon the beard, even Aaron's beard".) Through bringing the first-born to the priest, representing the Holy Elder, we initiate the birth of expanded consciousness so as to renew our energy as if we were born today — the idea of the Tefilin. This is because the whole power of renewal and long life comes from the Holy Elder who said he is very old but he still hasn't begun to live at all, as if he was born today.

This is the concept of Mashiach. Of Mashiach it is written: "I have given birth to you *today*" (Psalms 2:7). Mashiach will achieve this vitality to perfection, constantly starting afresh as if he was just born today. For Mashiach transcends time (see Likutey Moharan II:62). Similarly the boast of the Blind Beggar that for him the whole world is not worth the blink of an eye is the concept of beyond time. This is the long life the Mashiach will attain: "He asked of You *life* and you have given him" (Psalms 21:5).

King David and the Mashiach are one. This is why we say of King David, "*David melech Yisrael chai vekayam* — David King of Israel is *alive* and enduring". This connects with the teaching that the source of the kingship of Mashiach is the Tefilin, specifically the knot of the Tefilin (see Likutey Moharan I:54). Of King David, the Mashiach, it is written: "The soul of my lord shall be bound in the bond of life" (I Samuel 25:29). This bond is the knot of the Tefilin, which are life.

The length of the *retzuot*

[16] The two ends of the *retzu'a* of the Head Tefilin hang down in front over the chest: on the right hand side the *retzu'a* must reach down to at least the navel, and on the left hand side to the chest itself. (Some say that on the right hand side the *retzu'a* must reach down to the place of circumcision, and on the left to the navel. See Shulchan Aruch, Orach Chayim 27:11.)

Why the navel? We have seen that the holiness of the Tefilin derives from those elders who reached such a level of purity that they could remember what happened to them even at the time of the birth process, when the umbilical cord was cut. The cutting of the umbilical cord marks the conclusion of the birth process, and birth — renewal — is the main idea of the Tefilin. Birth is mentioned in the first of the parshiyot, which says: "Sanctify unto Me all the first- born, whatever opens the womb among the Children of Israel."

Of the Exodus from Egypt, it is written: "As for your birth, on the day of your birth your navel was not cut" (Ezekiel 16:4). In other words, before the Children of Israel came out of Egypt they were like an embryo still in its mother's womb, whose cord is not yet cut. The Tefilin express the idea of the Exodus from Egypt — the completion of the birth process, marked by the cutting of the umbilical cord.

Even though the other elders could remember much further back, it is not possible to reveal the holiness they achieved on the outside. The only thing that can be revealed on the outside is the level achieved by the first elder, who remembered being born — the cutting of the umbilical cord — as alluded to in the *retzu'a*, which reaches down to the navel. If only we could attain the level of this elder! But the levels of awareness achieved by the other holy elders are not revealed on the outside at all: their light is completely concealed in the *parshiyot*, which are hidden away inside the *batim*. From there we can only draw from their holiness in a concealed way, because the holiness of their levels of memory is far above us.

[17] The left hand side of the *retzu'a* must reach down to at least the chest. This is where the heart is located.

We have seen how the *retzu'a* is the light we draw from the divine attribute of patience. We have to draw it right into our hearts until we are inculcated with patience through and through and conquer our anger so thoroughly that we never take offence at anything, not even in our heart.

That is true patience, as the Rebbe said of himself after his journey to Eretz Yisrael. He said that in Israel he attained such a level of equanimity and patience that even in his heart he no longer harbored even the slightest anger even against his worst enemy, in spite of all the suffering he had caused him. The Rebbe still had absolutely no ill feelings against him (Shevachay HaRan #22). This is true patience and long-suffering — and this is why the *retzu'a* has to reach the heart: so that we bring this patience right into the heart, until nothing has the power to upset us.

III

David, King of Israel, lives!

[18] In the Song of Songs, God says to the Assembly of Israel: "Your navel is like a round goblet — rounded like the moon — in which there is no lack of blended wine" (Song of Songs 7:3). The Rabbis interpreted this as a reference to the Sanhedrin, whose seventy members used to sit in a circle like the moon (Sanhedrin 37).

The *retzu'a* of the Head Tefilin reaches from the knot at the back of the head down to the navel. The knot — in the form of the Hebrew letter Dalet — alludes to the kingship of King David, the Mashiach, who is "alive and enduring". The *retzu'a* extends from this knot down to the navel — namely the Sanhedrin. Its seventy members correspond to the seventy faces of the Torah. Now King David sat at the head of the Sanhedrin (see Rashi on Samuel II,23:8). The seventy members of the Sanhedrin — and the seventy faces of the Torah — all receive from David, the Mashiach, while his vitality in turn comes from the Holy Elders in the Story of the Blind Beggar, all of whom represent the various aspects of the Holy Beard. King David lived for seventy years. In addition, he slept very little: King David "never slept more than sixty breaths, in order not to have a taste of death" (Succah 26.) — because sleep is a sixtieth part of death (Berachot 57b).

Death came into the world because of the sin of Adam when he ate the fruit of the Tree of the Knowledge of Good and Evil. In doing so he cut himself off from the Tree of Life — and the Tree of Life *is* the Tefilin. We have seen that the Tefilin are *life*, and similarly, it is written of the Tree of

Life: "in case he should eat and *live* for ever" (Genesis 3:22). Because of Adam's sin the decree of death was passed on him and all his generations.

However, now that the sin has been committed, sleep and death are in fact very beneficial. If Adam had not sinned, he would have attained the *real* long life — eternal life — while still in his body. Even in his physical body he would have been able to be merged eternally in the Infinite, constantly renewing his vitality like the Supernal Elder, the Blind Beggar, who had a really long life and was always old and always young. However because of Adam's sin, the filth of the serpent gained a hold over his body, and as a result it was impossible for him to live eternally in his body. The only way he could achieve eternal life was through dying.

Death is therefore a great benefit, as the Rabbis commented on the words "And God saw everything that He had made, and it was *very* good" (Genesis 1:31). " '*Very* good' refers to death" (Bereshit Rabbah 9). For through death, which is itself a "sleep", the mind and soul are renewed, and the body is also purified and its vital powers renewed. One can then rise at the time of the resurrection in a pure, translucent body — a body cleansed and purified of the filth of the serpent. One will then receive new soul-powers and new levels of consciousness from the Tree of Life, the Tefilin.

This is how we will be able to live for ever — through constantly adding new life and new vitality. Eternal life cannot mean perpetual pleasure, because pleasure that is permanent and unchanging is not pleasure. A life of such "pleasure" could not really be called life. Long life in the true sense of the term is when one is constantly living new life: this is the long life — the eternal life — that will be granted in time to come after the resurrection of the dead.

[19] And even in this world the Tzaddikim who truly serve God can experience this eternal life through Torah, prayer

and good deeds. Their whole aim is to constantly renew themselves by adding extra holiness and attaining new levels of consciousness and vitality. Nevertheless, in this world it is impossible to live this long life without a break. Inevitably the mind tires, and one is forced to sleep. And sleep is in fact very beneficial. Through letting go of the conscious mind and sleeping a little, the mind is relaxed, and then it returns, renewed and refreshed, in the morning, and one starts living anew.

This will help us understand why we put on the Tefilin in the morning after having been asleep. In the Kabbalah teachings about the inner meaning and intentions of the Tefilin, we find that it is through going to sleep during the first part of the night, then rising at midnight to engage in Torah, that the lights of the Tefilin shine through in the morning. These "lights" are the residues of yesterday's consciousness, renewed during sleep. Then, in the morning they shine fully, and we receive a new state of expanded consciousness at the time of the morning prayers (P'ri Etz Chayim, Sha'ar HaTefilin, Ch.1). We will discuss these ideas more fully and elucidate them in the coming pages.

If you examine the section on the Tefilin in the Etz Chaim, you will see that all the different teachings there have been worked into the present discussion in such a way that everyone on every level and in every place and time will always be able to find new insipiration and fresh approaches to the service of God. Even the lowliest of people down will always be able to remind themselves of God's presence and love, no matter what situation they may find themselves in. This has already been discussed a little above, but "Give wisdom to the wise and he will become even wiser" (Proverbs 9:9). It is not possible to explain everything in writing. However with a little sense, someone who really wants the truth, and cares enough about himself not to want to deceive himself, will be able to get everlasting benefit from this discussion.

The Moon: Renewal

In our present state, then, it is not possible to live a life of constant renewal except through sleep. But the Tzaddikim sleep very litle, only as much as they need to in order to refresh their mind. This is why "David never slept more than sixty breaths" — because he lived this life of constant renewal and therefore slept no more than the minimum amount necessary for long life.

David's kingship is compared to the moon, which is constantly renewed each month. And the Assembly of Israel — the souls of the Jewish People collectively — are also compared to the moon. The Assembly of Israel is in fact the same idea as the kingship of David — King David rules over all the souls. Just as the moon is constantly renewed, so too the Assembly of Israel must constantly renew their service at all times in order to attain the destined renewal of the future and to live the truly long life.

Thus in the blessing to sanctify the moon, which we recite on seeing the new moon a few days after the beginning of each month, we say: "To the moon He said that it should renew itself as a crown of splendor for those He has supported from the womb [i.e. the Jewish People]. They are destined to renew themselves like it, and to glorify their Creator..." We follow the blessing with the words "David King of Israel is alive and enduring" (Orach Chayim 426:2).

The Jewish calendar follows the moon (see Chullin 60a) — a hint to us that we must constantly renew ourselves and live a new life every day and every moment in the service of God. We never ever get old even in a thousand years, because "a thousand years in Your eyes are like yesterday" (Psalms 90:4). For us, every day is new, because we measure our days by the moon. Each month the moon renews itself. The Hebrew word for month is ChoDeSh, from the root ChaDaSh, meaning new. At the beginning of each month we have Rosh Chodesh, literally the Head of the New, signifying the constant renewal of time. We then number all the days of the month from the New Moon — the second of the Chodesh, the third of the Chodesh, and so on. When we reach the end of the month, we start a new month. And so we continue. We measure all our days from the New Moon: renewal! All the days of the Jewish People, the Holy People, are therefore new and always full of vitality. And all this is because we have been given the Torah, the source of everlasting life: "For this is your life" (Deuteronomy 30:20).

[20] The Tefilin incorporate all these concepts. The knot of the Head Tefilin is bound up with the kingship of King David. From the knot, the *retzu'a* stretches down to the navel. This is where life begins. Only with the cutting of the umbilical cord does the child begin a new life as an independent person after leaving the mother's womb. The light of the Tefilin drawn down through the *retzu'ot* comes from the elder who remembered the cutting of the cord. He is the channel of the energy we need to constantly renew our lives as if we had just been born today and the umbilical cord was cut just now.

"The days of our years are seventy years" (Psalms 90:10). Our whole life is summed up in these seventy years. King David lived seventy years, corresponding to the seventy faces of the Torah. All the seventy faces — they are the vitality of the seventy years — derive from the Holy Elders, as we have seen, and the radiance of all of them is brought down to us by the smallest Elder of all, who remembers the cutting of the umbilical cord. The perceptions of the other elders, who are even more exalted, cannot be revealed outside.

"Your navel is like a round goblet..." (Song of Songs 7:3) — round like the moon, which is constantly renewed. This is an allusion to the seventy members of the Sanhedrin, corresponding to the seventy faces of the Torah and the seventy years of life we get from the Holy Elders through wearing the Tefilin. Their vitality is channelled down to us through the *retzu'a*, which extends to the navel. With this vitality we can constantly renew ourselves through all the seventy years of our life.

Someone who does not live this life of constant renewal will not live the full seventy years in the true sense of the word "live". To be alive really means to serve God — "for this is your life" (Deuteronomy 30:20). Someone who fails to add holiness and wisdom every day of their life will only have a short life. Even if they do live seventy physical years, who knows if all seventy will add up to even a single day of real life! This is why the wicked, who do not keep the Torah at all, are called dead even in their lifetime. They really are dead, because they are not fulfilling the Torah, which is the source of true life — for "this is your life". When someone serves God just a little, only their few good deeds and acts of devotion count as the days of their life. It could be that their entire life only adds up to a single day. Real life is the life of King David, who lived seventy full years, with new life all the time.

The Great Turnabout

[21] For David really had no life at all. He was too pure for this world. He was supposed to have been still-born, and he would have been, if not that Adam gave him seventy years of his own life (Zohar I:55a) and this was how David came into the world. Adam's life came from *Arich Anpin*, the "Long Face" — this is the term for the unitary Divine Will which is the source of all the details of the Creation. *Arich Anpin*, which is identified with the Divine Attribute of patience we have been discussing, is the source of created time and of holy vitality. This is the source of King David's life.

For David, everything was turned around — for good. At first he had no life at all: he was supposed to have been still-born. But then he was granted seventy years of the life of

Adam, and he lived all seventy of them as if he had never lived at all, as if he was just born today. He was like an aborted child every moment of his life. The aborted child has no life and has to receive new life through God's lovingkindness. This was how David lived all his seventy years, fighting unremittingly to add constantly to his wisdom and holiness. As a result, he attained long life for all time, because "David King of Israel is alive and enduring."

This is the life we get from the Tefilin. The word TeFiLiN is from the same root as veNiF'LiNu in the verse "*We are distinguished*, I and Your people, from all the people that are on the face of the earth" (Exodus 33:16). Moses said this at the time God revealed the Thirteen Attributes of Lovingkindness, in which the Tefilin are rooted. It was then that He said to Moses, "and you will see My back", which the Sages explained as a reference to the knot of the Tefilin (Berachot 7). Here is where the soul of King David — the Mashiach — is rooted. He was supposed to be an aborted baby — in Hebrew this is a NeFeL. But things were reversed and he constantly had new life, as if he was just born today.

"We are distinguished, I and Your people" — because things were reversed. From NeFel, an aborted child, came veNiFLinu, "we are distinguished" — the concept of the Tefilin, in which the underlying idea is the long life of King David. And Mashiach himself is called "Bar NiFLei" — an untimely child, because Mashiach will also have this long life, for "I have given birth to you today" (Psalms 2:7).

God supports all who fall

[22] "God supports all who fall (haNoF'Lim) and straightens all who are bent" (Psalms 145:14). "Those who fall" are the people who fall away from serving God. He supports them and arouses them from their sleep through the Tzaddikim in each generation. These Tzaddikim are the embodiment of

David-Mashiach, who succeeded in transforming the NeFeL, the abortive child, into one with long life — by always starting to live afresh, the idea of the Tefilin. The Tzaddikim give life and strength to all the people who have fallen down spiritually, saving them from demoralization and despair and helping them to return to God. They can then transform their fall into a major ascent. This is in fact why people are pushed down in the first place — to bring them to make a whole new start.

Thus, supporting those who have fallen and keeping them from despair is itself the concept of David-Mashiach, for whom abortion was turned into long life. The fall itself is transformed into a major ascent. Rebbe Nachman explains that when a person falls from his level of service of God, this is something sent from Heaven. The apparent rejection is the first stage in bringing one closer. The purpose of the fall is to wake the person up and arouse him to make greater efforts to come closer to God. He has to start serving God all over again, as if he hadn't even begun yet. This is a fundamental principle in serving God. We literally have to begin again every day (Likutey Moharan I:261).

The redemption of the Jewish People as a whole will come about through David-Mashiach — quickly in our days! Then the whole Assembly of Israel will rise out of their fall. The Rabbis asked (Berachot 4) why, in the Psalm of Ashrei, King David included verses beginning with every letter of the Hebrew alphabet except Nun. They answered that he did not want to include the verse referring to the fall of Israel — "NoF'Loh — she has fallen, the maiden of Israel, and she will not rise again" (Amos 5:2). Nevertheless, they continued, through his prophetic spirit, David foresaw that this harsh judgement would eventually be imposed. So even though he left out the verse starting with Nun, he sweetened this very judgement in the verse that comes immediately after where this missing verse should have been. The verse beginning with the next letter of the Hebrew alphabet, Samech, is: "Somech — God *supports* all who fall (haNoF'Lim)..."

The "fall" of the Assembly of Israel is their fall from the service of God. For the redemption to come about, the Jewish People have to repent (Yoma 86b). This is why the main support of the Jewish People in their fall is King David. Through living the kind of long life he had, he has the power to vitalize, strengthen and support all who have fallen and to keep them from despair through showing them that God is with them and close to them. So "Do not rejoice over me, my enemy: even though I have fallen, I will arise; I may sit in darkness, but God is my light" (Micah 7:8) The decline gets transformed into the ultimate ascent.

IV

The Tefilin of the Head and the Arm

[25] When we put on the Tefilin in the morning, we start with the Arm Tefilin and then put on the Head Tefilin. We will now examine the meaning of the order in which the Tefilin are put on. We will do this by exploring the relationship between the Tzaddik and the Jewish People — for the Tzaddik parallels the Head Tefilin, and the Jewish People the Arm Tefilin.

Two of the main concepts in the sections that follow are Zer Anpin, *literally "The Small Countenance", and* Malchut, *kingship or sovreignty.* Zer Anpin *is comprised of the six Sefirot: Chessed, Gevurah, Tiferet, Netzach, Hod and Yesod. Together with* Malchut *these make up the seven lower Sefirot, with* Malchut *being the lowest. The Sefira of* Da'at *is above* Zer Anpin, *and radiates into it.* Zer Anpin *then radiates into* Malchut. *(Da'at itself, the knowledge and understanding of Godly power, comprises at times Chochmah and Binah, and at others Chessed and Gevurah.)*

Malchut, *the lowest of all the Sefirot, reveals God's power in all its details to all the created worlds, down to the very lowest.* Malchut *is characterized as the "female" aspect, receiving the Godly power radiated from the sefirot above it. The higher sefirot shine down to* Malchut *in a complete unity, and this is what is known as* Zer Anpin. Zer Anpin *is characterized as the "male" aspect.* Malchut *is associated with* Emunah — *the faith in God's power over the entire creation. It is also associated with* Knesset Yisrael, *the Assembly of Israel (i.e. the Jewish*

People, who believe in God), and with the Arm Tefilin.
Zer Anpin is associated with Da'at, *the knowledge and*
understanding of Godly power, which is on a higher level
than faith. Zer Anpin *is also associated with the Tzaddik,*
who radiates the knowledge of God to the Jewish People,
and with the Head Tefilin.

We have already mentioned (in #18 above) that the light
of the Tefilin is drawn down through first going to sleep at
night, and then rising at midnight in order to mourn over the
destruction of the Temple and study Torah until the time of
the morning prayers. Let us now examine these ideas in more
detail.

When we go to sleep, we entrust our mind and soul to
God in pure faith, and they are returned to us, renewed
and refreshed, when we wake up. It is through faith in God
that we see God's kingly power, and this is why faith is
identified with Malchut. Each night Malchut — the revelation
of Godliness — comes down into the lower worlds in order
to sift out and lift up the holy sparks that are trapped amidst
the forces hiding Godliness. These sparks are the holy souls
that have fallen because of their sins. Through the descent of
Malchut, these souls receive a revelation of God's presence:
thoughts of Teshuvah, repentance, come to them in order to
bring them back to God.

In the figurative language of Kabbalah, through rising at
midnight to mourn over the destruction of the Temple and
study Torah, the Tzaddikim elevate Malchut until she rises
up with the light of day and sits on the left arm, which is her
proper place. (The Arm Tefilin, associated with Malchut, are
worn on the left arm.) Then Zer Anpin, the Small Countenance,
radiates expanded consciousness back into Malchut, because
previously it had left her, and only a residue remained in
the heart of Zer Anpin. The expanded consciousness had left
her previously because spiritual perception is only fully present

during prayer. Afterwards, only a residue remains, and at night even this trace withdraws — except that it remains in the heart of Zer Anpin. This is the idea in the verse: "Place me as a seal on your heart and as a seal on your arm" (Song of Songs 8:6).

Now when Malchut returns to her place and Zer Anpin sees that the expanded consciousness of Malchut, Emunah, has been restored to her, he becomes jealous of her — "hard as the grave is jealousy" (ibid.) Zer Anpin then takes back his own expanded consciousness, which was renewed during the night — this is the consciousness of Da'at, knowledge and understanding. Here we have the concept of the Head Tefilin, which is associated with Zer Anpin and with the expanded consciousness of Da'at, knowledge and understanding, as opposed to the Arm Tefilin, which is associated wih Malchut and the expanded consciousness of Emunah, faith (P'ri Etz Chayim, Sha'ar HaTefilin, Ch.7). And as mentioned before, Zer Anpin corresponds to the Tzaddik, while Malchut corresponds to the Jewish People.

The Tzaddik and the Jewish People

Let us now try to throw light on the meaning of these teachings by examining the relationship between the True Tzaddik and the Jewish People. The Tzaddik is associated with the Head Tefilin and the Jewish People with the Arm Tefilin.

The True Tzaddik is the one who brings the expanded consciousness and vitality associated with the Tefilin into the world: the Tzaddikim *are* the life and brain of the world! The leading Tzaddik in each generation is referred to as Moses (thus in the Gemara we find that one sage would call another "Moses", cf. Shabbat 101), and Moses is the concept of Mashiach (Zohar I:25b). Moses is the embodiment of Da'at, Holy Knowledge — the knowledge and consciousness associated with the Tefilin (see Likutey Moharan I:38). The True Tzaddik is the "river coming out of Eden to water the garden, and from there it is split and becomes four heads" (Genesis 2:10). The "four heads" are the four parshiyot of the Tefilin — they are the "brain" of the Tefilin, drawn down in the "river coming out of Eden", the True Tzaddik.

The Tzaddik — the Head Tefilin — radiates spiritual understanding to the Jewish People, drawing them to God. As for the Jewish People — the Arm Tefilin — their perception of God is founded on faith. Faith is indeed the foundation on which the whole of Judaism depends. Thus the Rabbis taught that "Habakuk came and based them on one thing: 'The Tzaddik will live through his *faith*' (Habakuk 2:4)" (Macot 24).

The Jewish People are unable to receive from the expanded consciousness of the Tzaddik — Da'at — the way it is: the Tzaddik's spiritual perceptions are too exalted. In order to radiate to the People, the Tzaddik has to throw aside his own perceptions and go into what for him is a state of "sleep" in which not even a trace of his expanded consciousness remains. He is left with nothing but a residue of faith, which stays in his heart — "as a seal on your heart" (Song of Songs 8:6). It is this faith that he radiates to the people in order to sift out the sparks of Godliness which are trapped in the concealment. He has to lift up the souls of all those who have fallen because of their sins to the point where God has become hidden from them. The Tzaddik is obliged to bring himself down to their level, putting aside his own profound insights in order to instill these people with simple faith so as to bring them back to God. Thus Rabbi Nachman taught that the Tzaddik draws ordinary people to God through simple, everyday conversations and stories. This, for the Tzaddik, is a state of "sleep" which he enters in order to elevate the world.

Afterwards, when the Tzaddik wakes up from his "sleep"

together with all the lifted sparks — the returning souls — they must engage in Torah, prayer and devotion in order to rise to their proper place. This is the idea of putting on the Arm Tefilin, whereby Malchut sits on the left arm, as mentioned above. In their previous fallen state, all expanded consciousness had left the Jewish People, remaining only as a residue of faith in the heart of the Tzaddik — "like a seal on your heart", as we saw. But after having lifted up the souls and returned them to God through faith, the Tzaddik now radiates higher wisdom and understanding to them in order to strengthen them in their faith and encourage them in their devotions. He teaches them to pay no attention to all the obstacles and temptations in life, but to overcome everything through holy understanding — faith.

This holy understanding is symbolized by the Arm Tefilin, which is worn on the "weak hand" in order to overcome its weakness. The "weak hand" is the sum total of all the obstacles and temptations in life, which derive from God's aspect of severity. All of them are overcome through the knowledge which comes from faith — the knowledge that God is everywhere and that therefore there is no obstacle in the world that cannot be overcome. There is no despair! There is no fall that one cannot rise out of. Through radiating this knowledge, the Tzaddik strengthens the souls he has lifted up until they are able to overcome all the obstacles standing in their way and draw closer to God, starting afresh each time.

Then when the Tzaddik sees the Arm Tefilin — when he sees his success in inculcating the people with faith and knowledge, because now they are strong enough to be able to stand their ground and overcome all obstacles — the Tzaddik becomes jealous of his pupils, as it were. For "from my students I have learned more than from everyone else" (Makkot 10a). The Tzaddik now remembers himself and his own true level, and this prompts him to bring himself back to his own true level of expanded consciousness, which left him at the time of his "sleep". His expanded consciousness then returns, renewed and greatly enhanced — the Head Tefilin.

The Divine Names associated with the *Tefilin Shel Rosh*

[26] The Head Tefilin is associated with the three Divine names EKYK (21), YKVK (26), EKYK (21). The total numerical value of their letters is 68, the same as ChaYiYM, life — the life of the spirit. The Arm Tefilin is associated with the three names EKYK (21), YKVK (26), ADoNoY (65). The total numerical value of the letters of these names is 112 = YaBoK (P'ri Etz Chayim, Sha'ar HaTefilin, Ch.1, and see Sha'ar HaKavanot, Tefilin D'rush 2).

The name EKYK involves the idea of conception. Literally the word means, "I will be" — in the future. Rabbi Nachman explains (Likutey Moharan I:6) that EKYK is bound up with Teshuvah, repentance, because before a person returns to God, he cannot really be said to exist in the true sense of the word. Only when a person begins to return does he start preparing himself for existence in the true sense. He then comes into the category of EKYK — "I will be" or "I plan to be".

Rabbi Nachman tells us that it is even necessary to repent for one's repentance! This is because it could be that one's first efforts were inadequate. Even the Tzaddik who has already come to perfect Teshuvah still needs to repent for his earlier spiritual perceptions. Every time he reaches a new perception he repents — EKYK — over yesterday's perception because it was too materialistic and thus detracted from the true exaltedness of God. The True Tzaddik is therefore constantly in a state of repentance — EKYK — constantly striving after new and higher perceptions. This is his long life — a life in which the Tzaddik constantly starts living, because each day it is as if he had not started to live at all yet and has not even existed in the true meaning of the word. Only now does he begin to live and start preparing himself for existence.

This is why the Head Tefilin, which is associated with the Tzaddik, is bound up with the names EKYK YKVK EKYK, having the same numerical value as ChaYiYM — life. Each day the Tzaddik starts again with EKYK, conception — "I plan to be" — as if he had never yet existed until now. And this in itself is how he achieves a completely new perception. The new perception is YKVK, which is the name associated with expanded consciousness (Likutey Moharan I:6). Yet as soon as the Tzaddik attains this perception, he immediately casts it aside, yearning for an even higher perception. Only a residue of the first perception is left, and the Tzaddik begins his devotions again. This is the idea of the second EKYK — "I plan to be". Thus we have EKYK YKVK EKYK, because the Tzaddik is constantly moving to new levels of Teshuvah. The numerical value of these three names is ChaYiYM, life, because the essence of long life is to constantly begin to live anew.

The Divine Names associated with the *Tefilin shel Yad*

The Arm Tefilin, on the other hand, which is associated with the Jewish People, is bound up with the names EKYK YKVK ADoNoY. Ordinary people also need to start again each day — EKYK, "I plan to be". They too come to a perception of God — YKVK, as above. However afterwards, when the intensity of the perception leaves them, they are left with ADoNoY: this is the concept of Malchut, Emunah — the faith that God is the Master (ADoN) of everything. Emunah — ADoNoY — must always remain in a person: it is the "point" which never leaves one. Ordinary people have to be left with a residue of faith in order to press on with their service of God. Their main reason for having to renew their perception is in order to remain strong in their faith, which is the foundation of their whole life, as it is of all things. Through the residue of faith in ADoNoY, the

Master of everything, their mind is renewed and they can then overcome all their obstacles.

The Tzaddik, however, who is associated with the Head Tefilin, is always returning to the level of EKYK, because he lives the real long life and is always beginning to live anew. This is the idea of EKYK ASHER EKYK — "I will be that I will be" (Exodus 3:14) — a concept of repentance for one's earlier repentance. One constantly returns to the level of EKYK and to fresh life. The first EKYK — "I intend to be" — signifies how one begins living afresh and rising to a new perception, the perception of the Tefilin. And thus ASHeR has the same Hebrew letters as ROSH, head — alluding to the perceptions in the head, i.e. YKVK. Then afterwards the Tzaddik returns to the level of EKYK again, as he begins to yearn for an even higher perception: this is the idea of the second EKYK, as mentioned above.

Thus EKYK ASHER EKYK, "I will be that I will be" is the same idea as EKYK YKVK EKYK, the names associated with the Tefilin. For God revealed Himself as EKYK ASHER EKYK at the time of the Exodus from Egypt, the Exodus being one of the main ideas involved in the Tefilin, as discussed earlier.

Even the ordinary person must also aspire to both levels of perception, the level of the the Arm Tefilin and that of the Head Tefilin. When the intensity of one's perception leaves him, the residue of faith which stays in the heart brings one to rise to new understanding, to strengthen oneself with added faith, so as to return to the service of God. This is the idea of the Arm Tefilin, associated, as we have seen, with Malchut and Emunah. The numerical value of the letters of the associated names, EKYK YKVK ADoNoY, is 112, YaBoK, which is BoKY — skilled: because it takes skill to overcome all the obstacles in life as we saw above. Then, having attained the level of the Arm Tefilin — strong faith and determination — one becomes jealous of oneself, as it were, and strives for higher perception in order to have the strength to rise from level to level and always live new life. This is the idea of the Head Tefilin, associated with the names EKYK YKVK EKYK, ChaYYiM, life.

3. The Order of the Parshiyot

Frontal cross section of the Head Tefilin showing the four separate compartments of which it is comprised, each containing one out of the four *parshiyot* written on its own slip of parchment, as can be seen through the cutaway. After each slip is rolled up it is tied around with thread made of animal sinew and wrapped in a small piece of parchment which is then tied around on the outside with animal sinew.

The *parshiyot* are arranged in their compartments so that someone directly facing the wearer of the Tefilin could (theoretically) read them in the correct order reading from right to left as customary in Hebrew.

Rashi:

D   C   B   A

Rabbenu Tam:

C   D   B   A

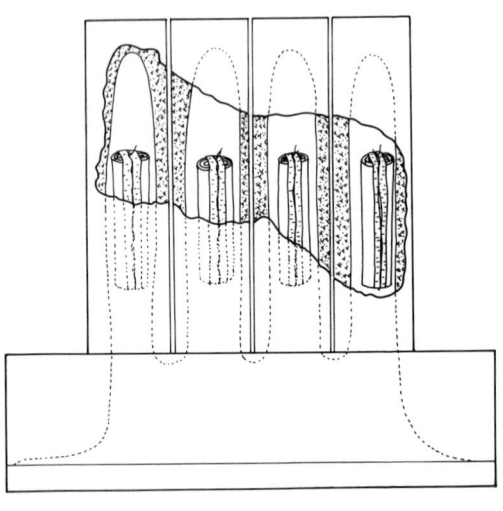

The generally accepted view as to the correct order of the *parshiyot* is that brought by Rashi, and all Jews wear Rashi Tefilin. In Rashi Tefilin the order of the *parshiyot* is (from right to left):—

A. "Sanctify" (Exodus 13:1-10); B. "When God will bring you" (Exodus 13:11-16); C. "Shema" (Deuteronomy 6:4-9); and D. "If you will listen" (Deuteronomy 11:13- 21).

A second view as to the correct order of the *parshiyot* is that brought by Rabbenu Tam. Rabbenu Tam Tefilin are worn by pious Jews in addition to their Rashi Tefilin. The order of *parshiyot* C and D is reversed. Thus in Rabbenu Tam Tefilin the order of the *parshiyot* is (from right to left):—

A. "Sanctify" (Exodus 13:1-10); B. "When God will bring you" (Exodus 13:11-16); D. "If you will listen" (Deuteronomy 11:13- 21); and C. "Shema" (Deuteronomy 6:4- 9).

(In the Hand Tefilin, where all four *parshiyot* are written on one slip of parchment, the order in which they appear also varies in accordance with the viewpoints of Rashi and Rabbenu Tam.)

V

Rashi and Rabbenu Tam Tefilin

The Talmud (Menachot 34b) asks in what order the parshiyot *are arranged in the Tefilin, and answers that A. "Sanctify" (Exodus 13:1-10) and B. "When God will bring you" (Exodus 13:11-16) are on one side, while C. "Shema" (Deuteronomy 6:4-9) and D. "If you will listen" (Deuteronomy 11:13-21) are on the other side. There is a difference of opinion between Rashi and Rabbenu Tam as to the order the latter two* parshiyot *are to be arranged in.*

The Tefilin all Jews wear are in accordance with the opinion of Rashi, and are referred to as Rashi Tefilin. In these Tefilin, the four parshiyot *are arranged in the* batim *in the same order as they appear in the Torah: "Sanctify", "When God will bring you", "Shema", and "If you will listen." However, the opinion of Rabbenu Tam is that "Shema" should be placed last, after the passage "If you will listen", instead of before it, as in Rashi Tefilin. Tefilin written according to this second view are known as Rabbenu Tam Tefilin.*

Many Jews wear Rabbenu Tam Tefilin in addition to Rashi Tefilin as an act of piety, in order to fulfil the mitzva according to both views. Some have the custom of wearing both pairs of Tefilin at the same time. However the more general custom is to wear Rashi Tefilin for the morning prayer service, and after taking them off to then put on Rabbenu Tam Tefilin.

[27] Each of the four *parshiyot* of the Tefilin is associated with one of the letters of the Tetragrammaton, YKVK. The first two

parshiyot, "Sanctify", and "When God will bring you", are associated respectively with the Yod — Chochmah (Wisdom) and the first Heh — Binah (Understanding). The *par'sha* of the "Shema" — the declaration of God's unity — corresponds to the letter Vav of the Divine Name. This is associated with Zer Anpin and the downward flow of revelation of God's unity and Lovingkindness into the worlds. The final *par'sha*, "If you will listen", describing the rewards for keeping the mitzvot and the punishments for breaking them, is associated with the final Heh of the Divine Name, corresponding to Malchut, God's kingly power — including the power to reward and punish. Malchut is thus associated with God's aspect of Strict Judgement.

In Rashi Tefilin the arrangement of the *parshiyot* corresponds to the arrangement of the four letters of the Name in order, YKVK. Thus in Rashi Tefilin, where "Shema" comes before "If you will listen", the Lovingkindness comes before the Strict Judgement. In Rabbenu Tam Tefilin, on the other hand, the placing of the *par'sha* "If you will listen" before the "Shema" corresponds to the arrangement of the letters of the Tetragrammaton as YKKV. The second Heh comes before the Vav — in other words, the Strict Judgement comes before the Lovingkindness. What does this signify?

Strict Judgement and Lovingkindness

The Rabbis teach that "God's initial thought was to create the world through the attribute of Judgement. But He saw that the world would not be able to endure, and He sent Lovingkindness first, putting it in partnership with Judgement: this is the meaning of: 'These are the generations of the Heavens and the Earth in their creation, on the day of the Lord God's making the Earth and the Heaven' (Genesis 2:4) — first 'Heaven and Earth', then 'Earth and Heaven'." (Bereshit Rabba 12:15)

The roots of the Sitra Achra, the Side of the Unholy, and man's evil inclination, which is a part of it, lie in God's aspect of Strict Judgement (Likutey Moharan I:72). In order to bring about the entire creation, it was necessary for God to conceal His infinite light, as otherwise there would have been no place for anything finite. The concealment of the light brought about the "Vacated Space" — vacated because it is apparently devoid of Godliness. It is in this Vacated Space that the finite creation came about. The hiding of Godliness is what gives man his free will and thus his challenge in life: in the absence of Divine light, the temptations of the evil inclination can seem very desirable, even though in reality they are evil, and end up causing those who succumb to them to be judged severely.

Man's ability to break his evil inclination is given to him through God's attribute of Lovingkindness, which He "put in partnership" with the attribute of Strict Judgement. This is what gives us the power to break the evil inclination and transform it into something holy. This is what is meant by the idea that the Tzaddikim turn the attribute of Judgement into Lovingkindness.

Why was "God's initial thought to create the world through the attribute of Judgement". Because He wanted man to develop such a level of determination in his service that he would have the power to break the evil inclination, rooted in the attribute of Judgement, *without* help from above. However God saw that it would be impossible for the majority of people to stand up to such a test and "He sent Lovingkindness first, putting it in partnership with Judgement".

This is why God is constantly taking pity on people and sending them thoughts of repentance so as to help them break the evil inclination. "Every day a person's inclination attacks him — and if it were not for God's help, he would fall into its power" (Kiddushin 30). The reason why "every day a person's inclination attacks him" is because of "God's initial thought...

to create the world through the attribute of Judgement." Every day the attribute of Judgement is stirred up anew, and this is where the daily attacks of the evil inclination stem from. But God immediately shows compassion and "sends Lovingkindness first" — in the form of the help He gives us each day to break the evil inclination. He sees "that the world would not be able to endure, and He sends Lovingkindness first."

The Greatest Tzaddikim

However there are Tzaddikim who are so great that they do not need help from above. In their case God sends Judgement first, yet they stand up through all the tests even though they have to endure all kinds of pain and suffering. Nevertheless they remain firm and thereby reach the greatest spiritual heights. We find that Jacob speaks of "God [Elokim] whom my fathers walked before" (Genesis 48:15). Elokim is the divine name associated with Judgement. Thus Abraham, Jacob's grandfather, walked before God by himself, without help from above (see Rashi on Genesis 5:9).

This explains the great suffering of so many Tzaddikim. "God tries the Tzaddikim" (Psalms 11:5) — like the flax-seller who knows he has good flax. The better it is, the more he beats it (Bereshit Rabbah 32). "God chastises someone he loves" (Proverbs 3:12). The work of the Tzaddikim is to sweeten the Strict Judgement at its root, which is the Initial Thought. They believe and know that the suffering and harsh judgements they endure are actually very beneficial. And their efforts bring them to rise until they become merged with the Initial Thought.

Thus when Moses saw how Rabbi Akiva was destined to be flayed alive with iron combs, he asked "Is this Torah? Is this its reward?" God replied "Be silent. This is how the thought arose" (Menachot 29b). The suffering of Tzaddikim like Rabbi

Akiva and other great martyrs derives from the Initial Thought whereby God wanted to create the world through Judgement so that man should stand up to the test without help from above and be merged with the Initial Thought. But God saw that the world could not endure, and sent Lovingkindness first. This way everyone has the power to break the evil inclination with help from above. Nevertheless great Tzaddikim like Rabbi Akiva and his companions serve God the way it first arose in God's thought, through Judgement alone. They suffer all kinds of pain and stand up through all the tests — and are thus able to rise up and become merged with the Initial Thought. "This is how the thought arose."

[28] We have already touched on the idea that the attribute of Judgement derives from the initial "contraction" of God's light which brought about the Vacated Space. The Vacated Space is the source of the deepest riddles of existence — issues which are unanswerable rationally, such as why the righteous suffer. However the great Tzaddik — the Moses figure — is able to go into these questions: this is the idea discussed above, of how the Tzaddik rises to the level of the Initial Thought. Through standing up to the tests and accepting pain and suffering, the Tzaddik is able to penetrate the secret of the Vacated Space and know that even within the concealment, God is hidden in the most awesome and amazing way — something that cannot be understood through human reason (see Likutey Moharan I:64).

The level of perception of these Tzaddikim is very exalted, and this is the level of perception associated with Rabbenu Tam Tefilin, where, as we have seen, Judgement comes before Lovingkindness. These Tzaddikim face God's Strict Judgement before they penetrate to His abundant Lovingkindness. This was how God originally intended to govern the world. These Tzaddikim thus become merged with the Initial Thought, and are able to sweeten all the harsh judgements at their very root. They achieve their heights through Judgement itself: by enduring so much, they succeed even by the criteria of the attribute of Judgement.

In Rashi Tefilin, on the other hand, the Lovingkindness comes before the Strict Judgement — in accordance with the idea that "He sent Lovingkindness first, putting it into partnership with Judgement". This is how God runs the whole of the rest of the world. And this is why the accepted way to fulfil the mitzva of Tefilin is with Rashi Tefilin, which are the only Tefilin most people wear.

However those who wish to sanctify themselves further must put on Rabenu Tam Tefilin as well, in order to receive added illumination from the exalted Tzaddikim who succeeded in rising to the Initial Thought thereby sweetening all harsh judgements at their very root. Rebbe Nachman thus encouraged his followers to wear Rabenu Tam Tefilin (Kochvey Ohr p.80, #36). The whole reason for our distance from God is because of the Evil Inclination. This is rooted in the Vacated Space as explained above. That is the level the most exalted Tzaddikim rise to in order to sweeten all the harsh judgements at their source. Through their achievments, even those who are far from God become able to break the Evil Inclination, which stems from the Vacated Space. That is why achieving greater holiness is linked to putting on Rabenu Tam Tefilin.

On the threshold of Mashiach

[29] In the present period, at the end of the Exile, on the threshold of Mashiach, it is especially important to put on Rabbenu Tam Tefilin, as emphasized by the great leaders of our time. For the attacks of the Evil One are stronger than ever now, because he sees that his end is very near. It is like when two people are wrestling and one sees that the other is getting the upper hand and is about to throw him down: he fights back with all his strength — because "no one is as strong as someone in despair".

The exile is "conception" and the redemption is "birth". The Exodus from Egypt was a birth: "As for your birth, on the day you were born..." (Ezekiel 16:4) And of the final redemption it is written: "For Zion travailed and brought forth her children" (Isaiah 66:8) and "Shall I bring to the birth and not cause to bring forth?" (ibid.9.) The end of the exile is marked by an intensification of the darkness. This was the case in Egypt, where Pharaoh gave instructions that "heavier work must be laid on the people" (Exodus 5:9), causing Moses to complain that "from the moment I came into Pharaoh to speak in Your name he has done evil to this people" (Exodus 5:23) The intensification of the exile at the end parallels the pain of childbirth — "And it was when Pharaoh made things hard before sending us" (Exodus 13:15).

All our present pain and suffering exile are birthpangs as we reach the end of the exile — "Like an expectant woman getting near to the time of delivery, who is in pain and cries out in her pangs" (Isaiah 26:17). The worst part of the exile is the attack of the Evil One against Jewish souls, trying to distance them from God. The suffering of the soul is the essence of the exile — everything else is vanity. The Evil One works hard to try to bring atheism into the world. The Rebbe said that great atheism is coming into the world, and we see it with our own eyes (Rabbi Nachman's Wisdom #220). Never in all of Jewish history has atheism been as widespread among the Jews as now, when so many have abandoned Jewish practice and become assimilated.

This attack of Evil is part of the birthpangs of Mashiach. The whole power of the Evil One comes from the root of Strict Judgement, the Vacated Space. Therefore, today, our only way to stand up against the evil is through relying on the strength of the truly great Tzaddikim, who have the power to go into the Vacated Space and sweeten the Judgement at its source. Since this is the source of the Evil Inclination, the Evil Inclination of everyone in the world is thereby quashed.

This explains the importance of putting on Rabbenu Tam Tefilin in our time. They bring us the expanded consciousness of these great Tzaddikim and give us the strength to repel the present attacks of the Evil Inclination and break it completely.

The Firstborn — on a deeper level

[30] The personification of atheism and disbelief is Amalek. Amalek is called "first of the nations" (Numbers 24:20). The reason is bound up with the Vacated Space, which is where Amalek is rooted, because the Vacated Space is the source of atheism. The Vacated Space came into being before the creation of the Universe, because without it there would have been no place for the universe. Without the concealment of God's infinite light, the finite world could not have come into being — the brightness of the infinite light would have made it impossible for the finite world to exist independently (see Likutey Moharan I:64). But because the Vacated Space conceals Godliness, it is the source of the kelipot — these are the "husks" that cover over and conceal the Godliness like the husk covers over the fruit. The husk comes first — you encounter the husk before you reach the fruit inside. Thus the Vacated Space came first, before the Universe, and because of this Amalek is also called "first", because his power derives from the Vacated Space.

Esau was the grandfather of Amalek and represents the same idea. Esau was the "firstborn" in the same way that the husks come first, before the fruit. Esau is rooted in the Vacated Space, which came first, before the world. Yet the truth is that God preceded everything, for God "fills all the worlds and encompasses all the worlds". He Himself brought about the Vacated Space in order to make a place for the creation of the world. And the Jewish People, through belief in God, who preceeded everything, are able to rise above all the idolatrous and atheistic ideologies which arise out of the Vacated Space. We have faith that even in the Vacated

Space, God is present, albeit concealed, because He preceeded everything. The Jews are called Hebrews — IVRim, from the root EVeR signifying passing over, because through their faith the Jews *pass over* and rise above all the ideological systems coming from the Vacated Space.

The Jewish People are therefore the true firstborn — "My firstborn son, Israel" (Exodus 4:22) — because through their faith they pass beyond the Vacated Space and believe in God Himself, who was the first and preceeded everything. This explains why Jacob took the birthright from Esau. At first the birthright had to be in the hands of Esau, because "the husk preceeds the fruit". Esau's birthright derives from the Vacated Space, which preceeded the world. But Jacob, through his faith, was able to transcend the Vacated Space and believe in and become merged with God, who preceeded everything. This way he was later able to cancel the birthright of Esau-Amalek — "first of the nations" — and take the birthright for himself — "My firstborn son, Israel".

This explains why the plague of the firstborn of Egypt and the sanctification of the firstborn of Israel came precisely at the moment of the Exodus. They were an integral part of the Exodus. The exile in Egypt encompasses all the exiles of the Jewish People, all of which derive from the impure influence of Amalek — the serpent. Amalek, "first of the nations", is the root of the four kingdoms under whose sovereignty the Jewish People have come (see Likutey Moharan I:30) and Edom, who is Esau-Amalek, was the guardian angel of Egypt. Pharaoh's stubborn refusal to let the Jewish People go came essentially from his atheism and disbelief, which derive from the Vacated Space — where Amalek is rooted. Thus Rabbi Nachman explains that Pharaoh is associated with the Vacated Space, which is the root of the heaviness of the heart — Pharaoh repeatedly "hardened his heart" (Likutey Moharan I:64).

"And it was when Pharaoh made things hard before sending us..." (Exodus 13:15) — this is the hardship of the birth process. Then "...God slew all the firstborn in the land of Egypt" (ibid.) in order to break the pride of the firstborn of the Other Side, who owe their position to the birthright of Esau-Amalek, "first among the nations" — a birthright rooted in the atheism deriving from the Vacated Space which preceeded the world. The purpose was to break the power of this atheism and give first place to the firstborn of Israel, who owe their position to the birthright of Jacob. For through his faith Jacob was able to transcend the Vacated Space and overcome all the riddles, questions and baseless ideologies deriving from it. He attached himself to God, who was truly first and preceeded everything, and who is the source of the holy birthright.

This was how the Jewish People was born and came out of Egypt. The firstborn were then sanctified: they were to be given to the Priest, who receives his holiness from the Supreme Elder (ZaKeN) on the side of the Holy, the "Beard (ZaKaN) of Aaron", as discussed above (see #15). The light of the Perfections of the Beard is brought down by the Blind One who became merged with the Infinite One — God was before everything, and in comparison with Him the entire world does not amount to the blink of an eye. The purpose of giving the firstborn to the priest is to sanctify the firstborn and draw into him the holiness of the birthright of Israel, which is Emunah. Through Emunah we pass beyond all other systems of thought and believe in God, who preceeded everything.

"And you shall *bring over to God* all that opens the womb" (ibid. v.12). The Hebrew word for "you shall bring over", *vehaAVaRta*, is from the same root as EVeR, discussed above, and is linked with the idea of transcendence. Through the holiness of the firstborn we are able to conquer the birthright of the Side of the Unholy — the Vacated Space. For through sanctifying the firstborn by giving him to the

Priest, we draw down on ourselves the perfect faith through which we transcend all alien thought systems.

We can now understand why the Exodus from Egypt, the sanctification of the firstborn, and faith are the main themes of the parshiyot of the Tefilin. They are all one subject, because through faith we transcend all the ideological systems deriving from the Vacated Space. This in itself is the essential idea of the Exodus from Egypt, which is integrally bound up with the sanctification of the firstborn.

Faith is the source of the vitality and spiritual renewal associated with the Tefilin. Faith is the source of life — for "In the light of the face of the King is life" (Proverbs 16:15). We believe that God created the world out of nothing and "in His goodness He renews the work of creation every day" (daily liturgy). "You made everything through wisdom" (Psalms 104:24): it was through wisdom that the whole creation came about. And it is through wisdom — the deepened understanding and added recognition of God that we have every new day — that the work of creation is renewed. "In His *goodness* He renews the work of creation" — "good is none other than Torah" (Berachot 5a) and "good is none other than the Tzaddik" (Yoma 38b) — namely the true Tzaddik who attains new understanding of Torah every day. Through this the work of creation is renewed, and this renewal is the essence of the Tefilin.

The Individual

[31] The birth of an individual Jewish soul is the same concept as the Exodus from Egypt. The birth of the individual is a triumph over the difficulties of labor, and so too the Exodus came about through God's overcoming the difficulties of the national birth by slaying the firstborn of Egypt. "When Pharaoh made things hard before sending us, God slew all the firstborn in the land of Egypt" (Exodus 13:15). The national birth which was the Exodus from Egypt was an awesome

revelation of how God constantly directs and renews the world. This was manifested in the plagues, the signs and wonders. Faith in God was precisely what Pharaoh was fighting against hardest. Pharaoh, who drew his power from Edom- Amalek, from the atheism of the Vacated Space, wanted to keep the Jewish People in their exile, and this was what made the birth difficult. "And it was when Pharaoh made things hard..." This was why God struck at all the firstborn of Egypt — the firstborn of the Other Side, the Atheism deriving from the Vacated Space.

Every Jewish soul is also a revelation. Each soul has a unique way of recognising "The One who spoke and the world came into being." For it is a basic principle that God never does one thing twice. Even when souls are reincarnated, the same soul does not come down into the world with the same combination of *nefesh*-soul, *ruach*-spirit and *neshama*-soul as before. There is always a completely new combination (see Rabbi Nachman's Wisdom p.163). So each time a Jewish soul is born, a new mind is born. The mind — the *sechel* — is actually the source of life and vitality: it *is* the soul, as it is written "the *soul* of the Eternal gives them *understanding*" (Job 32:8).

Each new soul that is born comes into the world in order to be able to know and acknowledge God in a new way. In every generation the souls are purified in particular ways in order to bring new understanding of God into the world. This is why God troubles Himself, as it were, to keep the world going from generation to generation. The purpose is to purify the souls more and more from the impurity of the serpent in order that they should come to a greater knowledge of God. "This is My name for ever, and this is My memorial to all the *generations*" (Exodus 3:15). "From generation to generation we will relate Your greatness" (Rosh Hashanah liturgy). "Generation to generation will praise Your works" (Psalms 145:4).

Therefore every time a new soul comes into the world, Amalek, the serpent, fights hard against it, trying to prevent the birth. This is why the birth process is so hard. The root cause of the difficulty was the serpent, who caused Adam to sin. Because of this it was decreed that "you will bring forth children in pain" (Genesis 3:16).

This throws light on Rebbe Nachman's statement that reciting the Psalm of Thanksgiving (Psalms 100) is beneficial for a woman who is having difficulties in childbirth. The subject of this Psalm is faith: "Know that HaShem is God" (v.3); "His faithfulness is from generation to generation" (v.5) — because faith is renewed and strengthened from generation to generation through the renewal of the souls — new minds perceiving and understanding God in new ways. The way to overcome the difficulties of childbirth is through faith. Faith and prayer are the same thing, which is why it is a Jewish custom to offer many prayers for a woman having difficulties giving birth. The difficulties stem from Amalek — atheism — trying to prevent the birth of a new soul that will bring added faith in God's renewal of the Creation.

The most powerful sign of God's renewal of the world is when a woman gives birth for the first time. That is when Amalek fights the hardest, and this is why it is necessary to sanctify the first-born by giving him to the Priest. This way we break the pride of the first-born of the Other Side — Amalek.

"God has a war against Amalek *from generation to generation*" (Exodus 17:16) Amalek fights in every generation, because he is the "old and foolish king" (Ecclesiastes 4:13). He does not want the renewal of vitality and understanding which comes about through the renewal of the souls in each generation, because he denies that God "in His goodness renews the work of creation every day."

The parshiot of the Tefilin begin with the concept of birth: "Sanctify all the firstborn to Me" (Exodus 13:2). The reason is that birth is the renewal of life and consciousness. This is the whole idea of the Tefilin — to renew one's mind and vitality every day in order to begin serving God each day afresh.

The Final Redemption

[32] The attacks of the Evil One are now stronger than ever as we reach the end of our present exile. Our present sufferings are literally birthpangs, the pangs of Mashiach. Our present difficulties are far harder than those at the time of the redemption from Egypt, because this will be the final and complete redemption: there will never be another exile. The filth of the serpent will be completely cleaned away and all Israel will return to God. The Revival of the Dead will then take place: the whole world will be renewed, and "He will swallow up death for ever" (Isaiah 25:8). Then we will live the long life of the Tefilin, the Tree of Life, for ever.

The reason the Evil One is attacking so strongly is because he sees that his end is near. His goal is to try to make the Jewish People old and tired, as if they have grown so old in this long exile, which has lasted nearly two thousand years, that there is no hope any more. He attacks each person individually with the thought that he has grown so old in his bad ways that he can no longer return to God — while the whole redemption "depends only on Teshuvah" (Tikkun 6, 22b). This is why we appeal to God: "Do not cast me off in the time of old age; when my strength fails, do not forsake me." (Psalms 71:9)

The prayer is that we should not fall into the old age of the Other Side. For the Evil One is called "old and foolish" (Ecclesiastes 4:13) because he denies that God is constantly renewing the world. This denial is the source of the old-old mentality of the Other Side — as if there is no way of renewing ourselves, God forbid. This atheistic idea, which is the main source of the power of the Evil Inclination, derives from the Vacated Space.

This is why it is so important to put on Rabbenu Tam

Tefilin today. The expanded consciousness they are associated with is that of the outstanding Tzaddikim who have the power to penetrate the very first contraction of the Vacated Space and sweeten the source of the harsh judgements. They "make His power known to the sons of men" (Psalms 145:12), showing that even the Vacated Space and all the riddles and questions it gives rise to are themselves derived from God, for He "gives life to everything" (Nehemiah 9:6). For it would be impossible to know anything of Him except through the withdrawal of light and knowledge which has to preceed our knowledge of God. The infinite light had to be concealed through the riddles and conundrums of the Vacated Space in order to make room for the creation of the finite world in which the knowledge of God could be revealed to finite creatures (see Likutey Moharan I:64). Through faith we break the husk which preceeds the fruit — the Vacated Space which preceeded the Universe. For through faith we transcend everything.

For this reason our main hope of getting out of this bitter exile and overcoming the birthpangs of the redemption, collective and individual, is through the strength of these outstanding Tzaddikim who have the level of perception of Rabenu Tam Tefilin. We must be especially careful to put on Rabbenu Tam Tefilin in order to bring the redemption closer — speedily in our days. This way each individual will attain the redemption of his soul and bring it out of its bitter exile amidst the worldly vanities that trap each of us in his own way.

One has to suffer the pangs of birth quite literally, especially at the start, and cry, scream, heave and sigh again and again until one is able to give birth to the holiness of his soul and redeem her from her exile (see Likutey Moharan II:4). This is how we will attain the complete collective redemption and quickly see the fulfilment of the prophecy: "Sing o barren, you who did not bear" (Isaiah 54:1). "Will I bring to the birth and not cause to bring forth?" (Isaiah 66:9) "For as soon as

Zion travailed, she brought forth her children" (ibid. v.8). Speedily in our days. Amen.

[33] This explains why in the morning prayers the prayer "U-vo le-Zion go'el" (And a redeemer will come to Zion) follows immediately after the recitation of Psalm 20 — "God will answer you on the day of distress". The Kabbalistic reason for reciting this Psalm is to give birth to the expanded consciousness and draw the influx of blessing into this world.

The Psalm has seventy words corresponding to the minimum of seventy cries a woman in labor has to emit before giving birth (Zohar III:249b). Sleep is pregnancy; waking up to a new day and starting one's devotions afresh is birth. The seventy voices correspond to the seventy faces of the Torah, all of which together make up the expanded consciousness we have to draw down into ourselves in order to wake up from our sleep — our spiritual fall. We have to recover the seventy faces of the Torah we have lost and start afresh. This is the essence of the redemption, individual and collective.

Immediately after the recital of Psalm 20 comes the prayer "And a redeemer will come to Zion and to those in Jacob who return from sin" (Isaiah 59:20). Those who "return from sin" are the Ba'alei Teshuvah, the penitents, who renew their former days which passed in darkness. "Turn us to You, God, and we will return; *renew* our days as of old" (Lamentations 5:21).

VI

Parchment and leather

The central concept in the following section is that of the ko'ach hamedameh. *Literally this means the capacity to liken one thing to another. For want of an exact English equivalent, the term is translated here as the imagination. It refers to the mental faculty through which we picture what the world is like. The* ko'ach hamedameh, *the imagination, is thus responsible for a considerable part of our mental life, in which our thinking and feeling, our attitudes and actions are founded on images, concepts, ideas and fantasies through which we view life and the world. The* ko'ach hamedameh *is contrasted with* sechel, *true knowledge of the essential reality of the universe based upon* chochmah, binah *and* da'at — *wisdom, understanding and knowledge.*

The images produced by the ko'ach hamedameh *may or may not be close to reality. For example we might have an image of something tempting — tasty food or the like — as being good, when in reality it could be harmful to us. Yet the image may be so strong that we pursue it regardless. Another example would be having a particular image of what someone else is like or of some harm we think they have done to us without stopping to consider if the person really is that way or did intend their behavior the way we understood it. On a different level, we may use material pictures to try to grasp spiritual realities, as when we think of Paradise as a beautiful garden.*

Our ko'ach hamedameh *is a raw power that consists of bad as well as good, because our impressions of reality are often far from the truth, yet they dominate our thinking and cause us to act accordingly, often doing great harm. One of our main tasks in life is to purify the* ko'ach hamedameh, *to clarify our thinking and rid ourselves of false ideas and understandings. This we do by developing our* sechel, *the intellect or reason, in order to come to a true understanding of reality.*

[34] The Tefilin must be written on the skin of a ritually clean animal (Shulchan Aruch, Orach Chayim 32:12).

The skin of the body corresponds to the *ko'ach hamedameh*, the mind's image-making faculty — the imagination. The imagination is the outer garment of the *sechel*, the higher intellect: our thoughts and images are the external garb in which the life of the spirit actually manifests itself in our conscious mind. The three internal lights of the intellect are the *neshamah, ruach* and *nefesh*. They express themselves in our *chochmah, binah* and *da'at* — wisdom, understanding and knowledge, the three parts of the mind. These three parts of the mind are the spiritual counterparts of the bones, sinews and flesh of the body. Just as these inner components of the body are covered over by the skin, so the three parts of the mind are "covered over by" and expressed in the imagination.

The skin is the most exterior part of the body. It is outside the flesh and sinews, which give the skin its shape, and they in turn are exterior to the bones. Skin without bones, sinews and flesh would be formless and without purpose. Similarly the thoughts and images in the imagination are empty and valueless unless they are in accord with the higher spiritual truth of the *sechel*. The imagination is called the "externality of the externality" of the *sechel*, which is "small" in comparison to mature spiritual knowledge and expanded consciousness, which are called "great".

The imagination is the animal faculty in man — even an animal has images of what it wants and what it is afraid of. Our main work of purification and clarification in life is with the images in our minds. We have to strip away the "husks" — the illusions, fantasies, misconceptions, material desires and the like — that are embedded in our way of thinking.

Purification and clarification of the images we think with brings to greater faith. Faith is a matter of the view we take of the world in those areas where true knowledge — *sechel* — is beyond us. In contrast to true knowledge, faith is our picture of the way we believe things to be: faith is in the realm of the imagination. To have true faith is to have a picture that corresponds with the essential truth, a sign that the imagination has been developed to perfection (See Likutey Moharan II:8).

As long as the imagination is unpurified, a person is beset by material desires and has all kinds of doubts and questions about faith. He is confused, and his thoughts take him away from God and from attachment to the True Tzaddikim. The source of all these confused ideas is the Vacated Space, which is where the husks derive from (see #27 and #30 above). Their main hold is in the realm of the imagination.

The reason for writing Torah scrolls, Tefilin and Mezuzot on animal skin is bound up with purification of the imagination — the "skin" — in order to come to complete faith (we have seen that faith depends on the purity of the imagination). Purification of the imagination is through the spirit of prophecy — the influx of true knowledge from a higher realm (see Likutey Moharan II:8). The Torah as a whole, and the passages written in the Tefilin and on the Mezuzot, are true knowledge — prophetic spirit. By writing Torah passages on the skin of the animal, the imagination — the skin — is purified. For even though the imagination is the lowest level of consciousness, the expanded consciousness embodied in the Tefilin is so great that it has the power to purify even the "externality of the externality" and the "smallness of the smallness".

Fixing the Vessels

The Kabbalistic concept of the vessels is of central importance in the section that follows. The Hebrew term keli *(plural,* kelim*) can denote either a tool or instrument on the one hand, or a container on the other, and the use of the term in mystical literature exploits both meanings.*

God's purpose in the Creation is to reveal His infinite Godliness to finite creatures. In order to overcome the gulf between the infinite and the finite, it was necessary to fashion suitable means — suitable "tools" or "instruments" — to do the work. A vessel or container is used to hold a liquid and pass it to someone else, because the liquid itself cannot be held in the hand. Similarly, God's infinite light had to be contained in a "vessel" in order to be passed on and communicated to His creatures, who could otherwise not grasp it.

The letters, words and paragraphs of the Torah are holy vessels through which Godliness is communicated to the world. Even a child can grasp the words of the Torah. Yet they contain infinite layers upon layers of meanings. The mitzvot are also vessels: each mitzva, with its various details, can be performed in the finite world. Yet it carries a meaning and significance that go way beyond this world. The entire Torah and the 613 mitzvot express the attributes of Godliness — Lovingkindness, Strict Justice, etc. These attributes — the Ten Sefirot — are the means by which God reveals Himself to the Creation, and the term vessels usually refers to the Sefirot.

The purpose of the vessels is to reveal the Godly unity

that underlies all things. Therefore, to the extent that the vessels appear as independent entities in themselves, their purpose has not been achieved. They are "flawed". Yet our finite minds cannot initially grasp that the various different vessels, the various Sefirot, are anything but separate and independent of one another. The paradox, then, is that the vessels must first appear as independent and separate before their intrinsic unity as attributes of the One God can be revealed.

There are thus two phases in the revelation of the vessels. The first is called "the Breaking of the Vessels". The Infinite Light is too great for the finite mind to grasp, and the vessels "break" — in the sense that they can only be grasped as separate and independent, even though in essence they are a complete unity. The second phase is that of Tikkun, "fixing", to reveal the underlying unity. The fixing is accomplished by the fashioning of new and "stronger" vessels which have the power to convey the ultimate unity of God even to the finite mind. Since God is all-powerful, He is able to bring even the infinite and finite into a unity and thus fashion such vessels. Indeed the Godly light through which they are made is higher than the light of the vessels which "broke".

The teachings of the true Tzaddikim are vessels of the latter kind, fashioned to convey the most exalted Torah teachings through simple, graspable ideas and parables etc. which have been devised in such a way as to have the power to communicate the inner idea without in any way distorting its true meaning. Rebbe Nachman's stories are outstanding examples of such vessels.

The greater the Tzaddik the greater his power to fix. He can reach down to the lowest levels and purify even the "exterior", the "smallness" — the levels which are furthest from the inner spiritual face. [In general, every level is called "inner" in relation to the level below it, and "outer" or "external" in relation to the level above it.] Through this power of the Tzaddik, all the worlds are fixed and all the scattered sparks and fallen souls are lifted up. The main hold of the husks is in these outer realms, but the Tzaddik has the strength to undermine their power completely.

The smallest of the elders in the story of the Blind Beggar remembered the cutting of the umbilical cord. Cutting the umbilical cord signifies the fixing and purification of the "skin": the umbilical cord, which is the link between the mother and the embryo, is nothing but skin. Similarly in the downward chain of the worlds, from world to world, the connection between a higher world and the world below it, deriving from it, is only from the navel and below (see Etz Chaim, Sha'ar HaNikudim. The start of a lower world in the world above it is from the navel of the higher world and below, i.e., from the beginning point of the Netzach-Hod- Yesod of the higher world — these are the "legs", its lower Sefirot. It is from here that the lower world derives its vitality, and so from world to world and from level to level.) This is why God arranged the creation in such a way that even the physical embryo should be attached to the mother from the navel, and the downward progression from one generation to the next, from father and mother to son and daughter, begins from the navel and below.

Similarly the exalted consciousness of all the holy elders is drawn down to us through the smallest of them all, the first starting from the bottom, who related that he remembered the cutting of the umbilical cord. For it is from the navel that the main revelation of the expanded consciousness comes forth and the downward progression of the worlds begins. This connects with the fact that the *retzu'ot*, through which we draw down the light of the Tefilin upon ourselves, reach down to the navel.

Yet although we receive the light only from the navel downwards through the bottom elder, who remembered the cutting of the umbilical cord, even so the inner vitality of the expanded consciousness we receive from here comes down to us only through the power of the highest elder, the Blind Beggar — the baby. For only through the power of the greatest holiness of all is it possible to fashion vessels which are capable of receiving the light even on the lowest levels.

Rabbi Nachman thus explains that in order for us to have some perception of Godliness on our human level, the Godly light has to go through numerous successive contractions as it comes down from above, level by level, from the higher intellect to the lower intellect, and so on. The lower a person's spiritual level and the greater the sickness of the soul, the greater the teacher he needs. The teacher has to be a master-craftsman, a doctor with the power to fashion vessels that can convey Godly perceptions even to someone that low (Likutey Moharan I:30).

This connects with the teaching in the Etz Chaim, Sha'ar HaNikudim etc. that the light of the vessels comes from a very exalted level indeed, and that the more exalted the level from which the vessels received their light, the less the breakage at the time of the "breaking of the vessels". For the higher and more exalted the light, the greater its power to contract and hide itself in such a way that the light is able to descend in a measured way without excess, and still bring about exalted perceptions of Godliness. The source of this exalted light is *Olam HaTikkun*, the World of Fixing, which derives from the level of 'Atik, the Ancient One. This is where all the elders have their hold.

The Supreme Elder was blind — he did not look at this world at all. Here we have the concept of the rectification of the eyes. It is from the Blind Beggar that all the others — corresponding to the eight *parshiyot* of the Tefilin — receive their vitality, down to the last one of all, who remembered the cutting of the umbilical cord, and through whom the light of the Tefilin is drawn down to us. (Thus it is explained in the

Sha'ar HaNikudim that the light of the eyes is revealed from the navel and below: the lights of the *nikudim* descended from the eyes and afterwards received lights from the point of the beard, and were then revealed from the navel and downwards — this is, in essence, the beginning of the formation of the vessels, whose purpose is to make it possible for Godly light to be apprehended even by finite creatures.)

This Supreme Elder did not look at this world in any way: he thus corrected the blemish of the eyes, which represents the sum total of all the sins of the Torah and is itself the concept of the breaking of the vessels. For all sins come about through the blemish of the eyes, as it is written, "And you shall not go about after your hearts and your eyes" (Numbers 15:39) — "the heart and the eyes are the two agents of sin" (Yerushalmi Berachot 1). Because this elder sanctified his eyes and closed them so as not to look at this world at all, the repair of the vessels which were broken because of the blemish of the eyes is accomplished through him. He is the Supreme Elder, which is the concept of 'Atik, through whom the repair is accomplished.

This is why the Tefilin are made of leather. Leather is skin, the "externality of the externality", the ultimate barrier dividing one creature from another and one world from another. It is from the skin that the light breaks forth. The light passes through the apertures in the skin to descend from world to world. The *parshiyot* of the Tefilin contain a total of forty-two holy names of God. (There are twenty-one names in the Head Tefilin and twenty-one in the Arm Tefilin. Together they correspond to the Name of Forty-Two Letters, which is the name God used in creating the world.) They are written on the physical skin of an animal in order to draw down the light from the highest, most exalted realm into lowly physical vessels, the "externality of the externality", namely the skin.

This enables us to receive the light of the perception of Godliness in a measured way through the fixing of the "externality of the externality" — the imagination — into which the light of perfect faith can now be brought. This is the essence of the holiness of the Tefilin. We receive this light from the Supreme Elder, who encompasses all the other elders and all aspects of the expanded consciousness associated with the Tefilin. Everything is fixed through this elder.

A clean species

[35] The skin used for the Tefilin has to be from a clean species of animal edible by Jews, even if the particular animal from which the skin comes was not fit for eating because it was not slaughtered correctly. In addition the leather has to be worked with the express purpose of being used for the mitzva of Tefilin (Orach Chaim 32:8, 12 & 37).

It is only possible to receive the expanded consciousness associated with the Tefilin if one works the skin of the body so thoroughly that not even the slightest trace of worldly desire remains — not even the faintest odor. The Rebbe once said we have to work the body so well that it is like leather you can turn over and see to be clean with your own eyes. He said there are great men who succeed in breaking their bodily desires but are still like leather which has a trace of a bad odor clinging to it. One has to purify and work the body so completely that not even the faintest odor of bodily desire remains. (Tzaddik #234)

Purifying the body is "working the skin", the "skin" being the imagination, which is the source of all our material desires. Those who purify their imagination completely attain the expanded consciousness in full and come to perfect faith — happy are they! As for ordinary people who fail to purify their bodies completely — and even great Tzaddikim do not always succeed — the remedy is to attach themselves to the True Tzaddikim, who through their own purity have achieved the holiness of expanded consciousness and prophetic spirit.

These Tzaddikim have the power to purify the imagination of the whole of the rest of the world to such a degree that everyone can come to perfect faith.

Nevertheless it is not enough just to attach oneself to the Tzaddik and wait for something to happen. One has to take the initiative and work on oneself — this is what is known as the "arousal from below" — because without this it is impossible to be lifted up against one's will. The main work is to give up one's own personal ideas and beliefs completely and listen very carefully to what the Tzaddik is saying. The Rebbe said that as long as a person still clings to his own ideas, he is not attached to the Tzaddik at all.

Moses called the Jews "a foolish people who are not wise" (Deuteronomy 32:6). The Aramaic Targum translates this as: "The people that received the Torah and were not clever". They were "not clever" in the sense that they threw away their own ideas completely, and this was how they were able to receive the Torah! If they had relied on their own theories they would not have been able to receive the Torah at all. The majority of people have no real grasp of intelligence in the true sense of the word *sechel*. This applies even to people who are pure and pious to some degree but have still not managed to break their material desires completely: the leather still has an odor! All their ideas come from the imagination, and as long as they have still not purified their bodies completely, their imagination remains animal and materialistic. This is why one must put his faith in the sages. The Jewish People thus "believed in God and in Moses His servant" (Exodus 14:31). One must attach himself to the True Tzaddikim with complete faith, putting aside all his own ideas as if he is completely devoid of intelligence.

This is the meaning of the law that Torah scrolls, Tefilin and Mezuzot may even be written on the skin of an animal that has not been slaughtered correctly, as long as it is from a clean species. This is to show that everyone can be lifted up so as to receive the expanded consciousness associated with the Tefilin, as long as they are in the category of the skin of a clean animal which has been worked for the express purpose of receiving the holiness of the Torah scroll, Tefilin and Mezuzot. This means they must work on themselves and strip themselves of all their own crooked ideas and opinions. They must prepare themselves body and soul to receive the holiness of the Tefilin — the expanded consciousness channelled by the Tzaddikim. They must accept what they teach just as it is, without turning aside to the right or the left.

This way even someone who has done a lot of wrong in his life can still receive the light of the Tefilin. He may be in the category of the skin of carrion as opposed to that of an animal that has been ritually slaughtered. Nevertheless, he can still receive the light — as long as he is not of an unclean species. This means one must not come to the Tzaddik with devious intentions, trying to test him and so on. One must not harbor impure thoughts in one's heart. This is the concept of an unclean species, because the root of uncleanliness is atheistic speculation, and atheistic ideas are symbolised by wild beasts of prey.

The *Batim*

[36] "Because the midwives feared God, He made them *houses* (batim)" (Exodus 1:21). These are the *batim*, the capsules, of the Tefilin. The Tefilin are bound up with the birth of expanded consciousness. The midwives are the ones who draw the light down, helping to bring about the "birth". We are told that the midwives *feared* God, because the Tefilin are associated with the fear of Heaven. Thus it is written that "all the peoples of the earth will see that the name of God is called upon you and they will be *afraid* of you" (Deuteronomy 28:10). The Rabbis taught that the name of God which the nations see on you is the Head Tefilin (Menachot 35b).

The midwives were Yocheved, mother of Moses and Aaron, and Miriam, their sister. Moses and Aaron embody the essential concepts of the Tefilin. Aaron the High Priest personifies the eight Perfections of the Beard — corresponding to the eight elders in the Story of the Blind Beggar and the eight *parshiot* of the Tefilin of the head and the arm. Moses is the Supreme Elder who boasted that he was very old yet still a suckling babe, and the whole world did not amount to the blink of an eye as far as he was concerned.

It is thus written of Moses, "And behold a young child was weeping" (Exodus 2:6). Even when Moses reached the perfection of holy old age, he was still young — a suckling babe: "I was a youth, and I am also become old" (Psalms 37:25). When the time came for Moses to die, "his eye was not dim nor was his natural force abated." (Deuteronomy 34:7) He was never senile in any way, even at the time of his death at the age of a hundred and twenty. Moses attained the ultimate in old age — where he was still completely young, as if he had not begun to live at all. He thus said at the end of his days, "You have *begun* to show Your servant Your greatness" (Deuteronomy 3:24) — as if he had so far seen nothing and God was only now beginning to show him His greatness. Moses constantly started afresh.

Moses is the concept of the Manna, of which it is written, "For they did not know what (MaH) it was" (Exodus 16:15). It is impossible to know "what it was" — what it really means for a mortal to attain what Moses did. The letters of the name MoSheH are Shin MaH. The Shin (numerically 300) alludes to the three Patriarchs, who are the sum of the expanded consciousness embodied in the Tefilin. However everything is drawn from the level of MaH — "they did not know *what* it was" — for this is the essence of Moses, this elder who was a complete babe. He is the root of everything and above everything, as it is written, "And the man Moses was very meek" (Numbers 12:3) — "...like a weaned child with his mother, my soul is with me like a weaned child" (Psalms 131:2). The Zohar tells us of Moses, that with the old he was old and with the young he was young — he was old and young at the same time.

At the end of his life Moses said: "I am a hundred and twenty years old today: I cannot go out and come in any more." (Deuteronomy 31:2) The Rabbis commented: "It was as if he was saying, 'Today my days and years are complete, for I cannot go further' — teaching us that the gates of wisdom were hidden from him that day." (Sotah 13b) The only way Moses could live was to have a life of constant advance. Once he could advance no further he had to leave the world (cf. Rabbi Nachman's Wisdom p.319). This is why "no man knows of his burial place" (Deuteronomy 34:6) — "For they did not know what it was".

Moses, then, is the Supreme Elder who is the root of the Tefilin, which are the beaming light of the skin of Moses' face (Exodus 34:35 — see Likutey Moharan I:38). His brother Aaron is the embodiment of the eight perfections of the beard — the eight *parshiyot* of the Tefilin, which are drawn from Moses. The midwives — Yocheved and Miriam — were the mother and sister of Aaron and Moses.

Now we can understand the meaning of the verse "He made them houses (batim)" (Exodus 1:21). The Midrash says these were "the houses of the priesthood and of royalty" (Shemot Rabbah 1), for Aaron was the High Priest while King David was descended from Miriam. The houses of the priesthood and royalty are the *batim* of the Tefilin. We have discussed above how the Tefilin are bound up with the priesthood and with kingship — *Malchut* — which is the concept of Emunah, faith.

The Tefilin embody the perceptions of Godliness which the True Tzaddikim, representing Moses, bring down to us through contracting and condensing the light. These Tzaddikim reach such an exalted level that they have the power to condense their perceptions and clothe them in many garments until we too are able to have some grasp of them. This is the underlying idea of the *batim* of the Tefilin. The only way we are able to apprehend the exalted light of the *parshiyot* themselves is through the *batim* and the *retzu'ot*. These are the vessels of *Olam HaTikkun*, the World of Fixing, which enable us to receive the Divine light in an ordered, balanced way. The great Tzaddikim have the power to penetrate the Vacated Space and reveal Godliness even there, and through this they are able to fashion holy vessels. The vessels are formed essentially through the fixing of the Vacated Space.

The Vacated Space was formed by the very first contraction of the light: this contraction is the source of all the screens and vessels in the whole system of Creation. They were all formed through the "thickening" and condensing of the light as it became distanced from the Emanator. Without the Vacated Space there would have been no "thickening" or "distancing" of the light. The formation of the vessels therefore stems essentially from the Vacated Space.

However as a result of the sin of Adam, the evil of the Vacated Space — atheism — got a hold on the vessels. It is the "skin", the "externality", of the vessels that gives them the appearance of being a plurality, independent of one another. This "skin" is the "skin of the serpent", where all the husks have their hold, and where evil has its strongest grip. This is the reason why the main rectification is through the working of the skin for holy purposes — purifying the imagination. This is the rectification of the Vacated Space accomplished by the great Tzaddikim to form holy vessels in which to receive the light in an orderly, balanced manner.

Torah scrolls and Tefilin are therefore written on the skin of a clean animal, as discussed above. And the *batim* of the Tefilin are made of leather — because the light can only be received by means of numerous contractions and vessels formed through the fixing of the Vacated Space — purification of the imagination, which is the "skin". Thus we find that after Adam's sin, "The Lord God made for Adam and his wife garments of *leather* and clothed them" (Genesis 3:21) — because the main thing to be fixed is the skin. The "garments of leather" are the Tallit and Tefilin: the Tefilin are made of leather, while the wool of the Tallit grows on the skin of the animal.

"And it came to pass, because the midwives *feared* God". It is through holy awe that the rectification of the contraction which caused the Vacated Space is accomplished. This contraction is the source of all severe judgements. The contraction is sweetened at its source through holy awe — holy judgement. "Because the midwives feared God He made them houses": it is through awe that the *batim* are formed, namely the vessels through which the light of the Tefilin is received in an orderly, balanced manner.

Sewing of the *batim* with animal sinews

[37] The *batim* of the tefilin have to be sewn up with threads made from animal sinews (Orach Chaim 32:49).

The reason for this is that even when the *parshiyot* are in the *batim*, it is only possible for us to receive the light when the *batim* are sewn closed. The purpose of this is to hide and mute the light so that it should not shine excessively, making it impossible for us to receive it.

The reason for sewing with animal sinews is because the sinews of the body — the blood vessels — involve the idea of limitation. The three hundred and sixty-five sinews of the body are the channels through which blood — the basis of life in man and all other creatures — flows. Vitality is constantly coming down from God, the Life of life, but we are only able to receive it in a measured way, through narrow channels. It is through the Torah, which is the name of the Holy One, blessed-be-He, that vitality is drawn down in a measured way into the vessels. And thus the three hundred and sixty-five sinews in the human body correspond to the three hundred and sixty-five prohibitions of the Torah, all of which are limitations deriving from the side of restraint, the side of Judgement.

Of the name of God it is written, "This is My name for ever and this is My memorial to all generations" (Exodus 3:15). The Hebrew for "My name" is Sh'MY. The numerical value of the letters of Sh'MY, together with YK — the first two letters of the Tetragrammaton — is three hundred and sixty-five. Now the name of a thing is the source of its vitality — for "the soul of a living thing, that is its name" (Genesis 2:19) — the soul of a thing, the source of its vitality, is identified with its name. Just as the name of person contains his whole vitality, so the Torah, the name of the Holy One, blessed-be-He, contains His vitality. Thus when we recite the words of the Torah, we are calling to God by His name and drawing His vitality into the vessels, i.e. the letters of the Torah, which are the name of God (see Likutey Moharan I:56).

This explains why the numerical value of the letters of Sh'MY, "My name", together with YK from the Tetragrammaton, is three hundred and sixty-five. The concept of the name as the limited channel through which vitality flows down from the Life of life is the same as that of the three hundred and sixty-five prohibitions of the Torah, which are restrictions and limitations by means of which the light can be received in a measured way. The three hundred and sixty-five days of the year involve the same concept: the vitality of all the days of the year is drawn down through the three hundred and sixty-five limited channels discussed above. By this means the life-force is drawn down in a measured way.

The Tefilin, as we have seen, are bound up with the concept of life. Life is drawn from the name of God, and the Tefilin themselves are called "the name of God". The Torah thus tells us that "All the peoples of the earth will see that the *name of God* is called upon you" (Deuteronomy 28:10), and as we have seen, the Rabbis understood this to refer to the Tefilin. The Tefilin must therefore be sewn with sinews in order to contract the light — the flow of life — so that it can be received in a graded manner.

In the verse quoted above, "This is My name for ever and this is My memorial to all generations" (Exodus 3:15), the Hebrew word for "My memorial" is ZiChRY. The numerical value of ZiChRY, together with VK — the last two letters of the Tetragrammaton — is 248. This is the number of positive commandments of the Torah, corresponding to the 248 bones in the male body. Now the two hundred and forty-eight positive commandments derive from the "right side", the side of Lovingkindness, while the three hundred and sixty-five prohibitions derive from the "left side", the side of Strict Judgement and restraint. Why then are the three hundred and sixty-five prohibitions alluded to in the first two letters of the Tetragrammaton, which are more exalted than the last two?

The reason is because the fixing of the vessels — the restricted channels — requires a higher light. Only this way is it possible to make God's greatness known to everyone in the world and to magnify His name in the mouths of all in order to speak of His name in all the earth (cf. Exodus 9:16). This fixing is accomplished through the Tefilin, which are bound up with a very exalted level of consciousness drawn down through many contractions, so that we and even all the other inhabitants of the world will know of God's name and might, "And all the peoples of the earth will see that the name of God is called upon you and they will be afraid of you" (Deuteronomy 28:10).

VII

The Ultimate Faith

[38] "And the life of Sarah was a hundred years and twenty years and seven years, the years of the life of Sarah" (Genesis 23:1) The fourfold repetition of the word "years" in this verse corresponds to the four *parshiyot* of the Tefilin, which are the main source of our vitality all the years of our lives. The Rabbis said of Sarah that "when she was a hundred she was like a woman of twenty, and when she was twenty she was like a girl of seven" (Bereshit Rabbah 58). Sarah thus had the perfect attitude to life, the approach we have been discussing, where one constantly starts afresh and even when advanced in years, still looks at oneself as being very young — a suckling babe — as if one hadn't even begun to live and serve God yet. One constantly starts afresh. "All the years of the life of Sarah were equally good" (ibid). Sarah's years were all good because she attained the *real* long life — the life of the Tefilin.

Sarah is the personification of Malchut, kingship, which is identified with Emunah, faith (we believe in God as the King). The association of Sarah with Malchut is implicit in Sarah's name, which denotes rulership. Thus the Rabbis said that "She ruled (Heb. = sara) over the whole world" (Berachot 13a), as it is written: "And God will be King over the whole earth" (Zechariah 14:9).

We saw earlier (#25) that when drawing down the expanded consciousness associated with the Tefilin, we start with the residue of Emunah which is left in the heart. Then afterwards, when the expanded consciousness has been drawn down, the

Emunah radiates with even greater light and perfection. For they depend on each other. Through Emunah we come to the expanded consciousness, and the expanded consciousness in turn helps us develop and strengthen our Emunah — and so the cycle continues.

By ascending from level to level, it is possible to reach such a degree of perfect Emunah that one comes to the highest Emunah of all, which is called the *Rosh Emunah* — "the Head of Emunah" (Song of Songs 4:8). This level is beyond anything we can grasp in our conscious minds, and is symbolized in the Head Tefilin. The Arm Tefilin correspond to "his *hands* were Emunah" (Exodus 17:12), while the Head Tefilin are "the *Head* of Emunah". The level of the Head of Emunah is beyond the expanded consciousness we have been discussing until now, which involves perception of the flow of Godly light through the revealed Sefirot. The Head of Emunah reaches out for the hidden Source, and can only be attained after one has achieved expanded consciousness in full and has a complete perception of the revealed Sefirot.

Every World includes the complete array of the Ten Sefirot from Atik, the highest, (also called Keter, the Crown), down to Malchut, the lowest. Now the Malchut of a higher World is above Atik of the World below it, and is actually its root. So it is from World to World. Now Malchut corresponds to Emunah, while Atik, which is the root and source of all the Sefirot in each World, involves the concept of will — the innermost will and desire to cling powerfully to God. (Atik, being itself the highest level, reaches ever higher, and is thus the concept of longing and desire.)

We see expressions of this desire in the Psalms: "My soul thirsts for You, my flesh longs for You" (Psalms 63:2). "My flesh and my heart fail, but God is the rock of my heart and my portion for ever" (ibid. 73:26). "My soul yearns and pines for the courts of HaShem, my heart and my flesh sing for joy to the living God" (ibid. 84:3). All his life King David prayed for this attachment: "One thing have I asked from God, that is what I seek, to gaze upon the pleasantness of God and visit daily in His temple" (Psalms 27:4). This is the attachment we attain through the Tefilin, of which it is written: "But you that are *attached* to the Lord your God are *alive* every one of you today" (Deuteronomy 4:4). For it is written of the Tefilin: "Set me as a seal upon your heart, as a seal upon your arm, for love is strong as death, jealousy is cruel as the grave, the flashes thereof are flashes of fire, a very flame of the Lord. Many waters cannot quench love, neither can the floods drown it..." (Song of Songs 8:6).

However there is a level of attachment which is below the level of Emunah of the higher level. Thus Atik of the World of Action (*Asiyah*, the lowest World) is below the Malchut-Emunah of the World above it, the World of Formation (*Yetzira*), and Atik of Asiyah is obviously lower than Malchut in the Worlds which are even higher. And so from World to World. This is why the essential starting point is always Emunah, and so too the end, the goal, is always Emunah and attachment. Because in actual fact everything is one. The desire and yearning of each World and level to rise higher — the Atik, the innermost desire of that World or level — is itself an illumination of the Emunah which is the lowest level of the World above it. For the Malchut-Emunah of the higher World is the source and the goal of the vitality of the Atik-desire of the World and level below it, and so on.

Try to understand this well, for in the light of this discussion you will be able to begin to get an initial understanding of the teachings of the Holy Zohar and the ARI z"l, and you will be able to derive practical guidance from them with the help of Rebbe Nachman's teachings. Each one of the Rebbe's lessons and stories is an introduction, opening many gateways to the understanding of Godliness. If you persist with his teachings and study and follow them day by day, you will eventually be able to understand all the pathways of the Kabbalah.

Thus, in essence, the expanded consciousness and vitality associated with the Tefilin are a radiation of Emunah developed to perfection stage by stage, as explained above. This is why the Tefilin are the "life of Sarah", the life of Malchut, Emunah, which is Sarah, "because she ruled over the whole world" — the concept of the revelation of His faith and His kingship over all the dwellers on earth — "And God will be King over the whole earth" (Zechariah 14:9).

The Cave of Machpelah

[39] The Cave of MaChPeLah gets its name from the couples (the Hebrew word CaPhuL means double) who are buried there — Adam and Eve, Abraham and Sarah, Isaac and Rebecca, and Jacob and Leah (see Eruvin 53). The town where the Cave is located is called Kiryat Arba — the City of Four, because of these four pairs. The four pairs correspond to the Head Tefilin and the Arm Tefilin: each of the four *parshiyot* in the one is paired with its counterpart in the other. As mentioned earlier, the four *parshiyot* of the Head Tefilin are associated with the male aspect of spiritual consciousness, while the four *parshiyot* of the Tefilin of the hand are associated with the female aspect (P'ri Etz Chayim, Sha'ar HaTefilin, Ch.5).

Machpelah also carries an allusion to the long life the Tzaddikim have: their holiness and vitality are constantly being doubled — because they keep on adding and adding to their existing holiness and devotion. "For double is the due of wisdom" (Job 11:6), "for all her house is clothed in scarlet (Hebrew = ShoNiM)" (Proverbs 31:21): ShoNiM is the same as ShNayiM, which means two — double! Thus in teaching us about charity, the essence of saintliness, the Torah repeatedly uses double expressions: "You shall surely open (FoTo'aCh tiFTaCh" (Deuteronomy 15:8), "You shall surely give (naToN tiTeN)" (ibid. v.10), and "You shall surely award (ha'ANeK ta'ANiK" (ibid. v.14; see Yalkut Shim'oni

Mishley 31). This is the concept of the Mishneh Torah — the repetition of the Torah (Deuteronomy 17:18). And "therefore in their land they will possess double" (Isaiah 61:7) — this is the concept of the eternal life which the Tzaddikim attain through constantly adding to and doubling their holiness at all times.

[40] Abraham purchased the Cave of Machpelah from Ephron. EPhRon is the concept of earth and dust — Heb. APhaR — namely evil, because evil is rooted in earth, the lowest and most material of the four elements of Creation. Evil is the serpent, and "As for the serpent, dust shall be his food" (Isaiah 65:25). Our experience of the "bite of the serpent" comes in the form of depression, laziness and heaviness (see Likutey Moharan I:189). The way to conquer them is through the holy aspect of the earth element, namely Emunah, faith. Emunah is called earth: "Dwell in the land and pasture off Emunah" (Psalms 37:3). The higher elements are only revealed through the earth element — this is the meaning of the saying that "Earth is the vessel of all things" (Tikkuney Zohar 70, 120b). And thus it is only through Emunah, the holy aspect of the earth element, that we draw down and receive vitality and all kinds of holiness. Emunah gives us the power to grow, sprout and blossom in our devotions and to overcome all obstacles and barriers. For Emunah is the power of growth and regeneration, the patience we have been discussing (see Likutey Moharan I:155).

Abraham bought the Cave of Machpelah from none other than Ephron, because the husk comes before the fruit. The Cave of Machpelah is the concept of long life, faith, growth and regeneration, — the very opposite of Ephron, who is the personification of death, depression and laziness — the serpent, for "God made the one (the side of impurity) opposite the other (the side of holiness)" (Ecclesiastes 7:14). Initially the Cave of Machpelah was in exile in the hands of Ephron.

It was Abraham, the first of all believers, who succeeded in taking this exalted holiness out of his hands. Abraham was able to do this because he achieved holy old age and long life: "And Abraham was old and advanced in days" (Genesis 24:1). For Abraham was the first to understand the holiness of Eretz Yisrael, which is the concept of Emunah, through which we achieve everything. This is why his first possession in Eretz Israel was the Cave of Machpelah. That is where we come to long life, the life of the Tefilin, which we attain through Emunah, the essence of the holiness of Eretz Israel.

VIII

A Narrow Bridge

[41] The *titura* of the Tefilin is the skin drawn over the bottom of the *batim*, the capsules, to close them after the *parshiyot* have been put in. The word *titura* actually means a bridge. The *ma'barta* (see above #11) comes off from the *titura*. The *titura* and the *ma'barta* are the only parts of the *batim* which are in actual contact with the body. The reason for this is because these two concepts are the most important aspects of the Tefilin we need in life. We need a bridge to help us get across this world in peace — to get over all the obstacles and distractions we face and come truly close to God.

The *titura* of the Tefilin, the bridge from which the *ma'barta* comes off, is connected with the idea that Jacob "passed over the ford of the Yabok... and he brought over that which he had" (Genesis 32:23-4). Rashi comments (ad loc.) that Jacob "made himself like a bridge" [i.e. he held both sides of the ford, allowing the others to cross over him]. The ford of the Yabok (ma'var Yabok) is the concept of the *ma'barta*, as discussed above. "And he brought over that which he had" — "he made himself like a bridge": here we have the concept of the *titura*, which is a bridge.

Jacob is truth: "You give truth to Jacob" (Micah 7:20). And truth is the underlying concept of the Tefilin (see Likutey Moharan I:47). For the Tefilin are bound up with Emunah, faith, and faith and truth are linked concepts: what we believe in is the truth (see Likutey Moharan I:7). The link between faith and truth is also seen in the comment of the Rabbis on "he bowed his head toward the earth" (Exodus 34:8) as discussed earlier (#6). "What did he see?" the Rabbis asked. "One Rabbi said he saw patience, and one Rabbi said he saw truth". The Gemara comments: "Each puts it in his own way, but there is no difference between the two teachings" (Sanhedrin 111). In other words, patience — which is Emunah — and truth are considered one.

"In this world a person has to cross over a narrow bridge, and the main thing is not to be afraid at all" (Likutey Moharan II:48). The way to cross the narrow bridge of this world is with the bridge of the Tefilin, namely through truth. And indeed it is a popular saying that with truth you can overcome the whole world. Truth is the most important thing of all, because truth is the seal of the Holy One, Blessed-be-He, and with it Heaven and Earth were stamped. The Torah opens with the words: "In the beginning God created" (Genesis 1:1). The last letters of the three words in the Hebrew are "BereshiT barA ElokiM", which spell out the word EMeT, truth. This is the foundation of the whole world and all its fullness. No matter what distractions and obstacles a person faces in his efforts to serve God — and the main obstacles are in one's own mind — the most important advice to overcome them all is to be truthful.

"Send Your light and Your truth, they will lead me" (Psalms 43:3). "I will go in Your truth" (ibid. 86:11). For truth is the bridge to holiness, and this is why Jacob — Truth — "made himself like a bridge". He did so in order to save all he had from the "terror by night" (Psalms 91:5), namely Esau, who was on his way towards him. Esau represents all the threats, problems and difficulties people suffer because of their various enemies and opponents, and the various obstacles created by the Evil Urge. Jacob was giving a sign to his children and descendants that the only way to overcome all these terrors is through truth. This is how we can get across the narrow bridge we have to cross without fear.

Similarly, at the splitting of the Red Sea, the sea turned into dry land until "the deeps were congealed in the heart of the sea" (Exodus 15:8) and God miraculously provided a bridge with which to cross the sea in peace. It came about through Jacob — truth — which is why the Psalmist says, "What was with you, sea, that you ran away? ... at the presence of the God of *Jacob*" (Psalms 114:5 and 7). Jacob is truth, and truth is our bridge even in the middle of the sea. "Thus says Your Creator: *Jacob*, do not fear, for when you cross over the waters, I am with you" (Isaiah 43:1-2). Through Jacob — truth — you do not have to fear when you go across the waters. With truth you can overcome everything and come through safely and in peace.

On the third day of the Creation, "God said, 'Let the waters under the heaven be gathered together in one place, and let the dry land appear' " (Genesis 1:9). For the third day is the concept of Jacob — the third Patriarch — truth — the bridge with which we are able to pass over the raging waters safely. This is the concept of the dry land which was formed in the middle of the waters at the time of the creation — this is a bridge across the world as a whole. It was made on the third day — corresponding to Jacob, who is the concept of truth. For truth is the bridge with which to cross over the whole world, and this is the meaning of the *titura*, the bridge, of the Tefilin.

[42] When putting on the Tefilin, after the Arm and Head Tefilin are in place, the final stage is to wind the *retzu'a* of the Arm Tefilin three times on the middle finger of the left hand. For the middle finger symbolizes Jacob, who is "the middle bar in the midst of the boards, which shall pass through from end to end" (Exodus 26:28. See Zohar III:227a; 228a-b). The *retzu'a* is bound on the *third* finger, because this is the concept of Jacob, truth.

Now that the Tefilin are in place, Emunah is complete.

While winding the *retzu'a* three times around the middle finger, we recite the verses from Hosea containing the threefold expression of betrothal: "I will betroth you to Me forever. I will betroth you to Me in righteousness and justice, in lovingkindness and compassion. I will betroth you to Me in *faith*, and you will *know* God" (Hosea 2:21-22). Emunah, faith, and Da'at, the knowledge of God, are interdependent. Emunah is mentioned first, because it is the basis of everything. The *retzu'a* is bound on the *third* finger corresponding to Jacob, truth, and Emunah depends on truth, as mentioned above.

"I will betroth you to Me *forever*" — this is the concept of long life, eternal life. "I will betroth you to Me in righteousness and justice, in lovingkindness and compassion." These four concepts are the crowning glory of the Tefilin — corresponding to the four *parshiyot* and the four *batim* of the Head Tefilin. Thus Rashi comments on this verse in Hosea that "the Holy One, blessed-be-He makes a crown out of all four of them on the head of Israel" — i.e. the Tefilin, which are the crown of the Jewish people. "I will betroth you to Me in faith" — because Emunah is the foundation and the goal of spiritual perfection.

Wrestlings with God

[43] The knot which is tied in the *retzu'a* next to the *bayit* of the Arm Tefilin is in the shape of the letter yod. The Arm Tefilin are symbolic of the support and encouragement needed by those who have fallen down spiritually, so as not to fall away completely. The knot in the form of the yod at the side of the Arm Tefilin represents the illumination from the Tzaddik, "foundation of the world" (Proverbs 10:25) to the Assembly of Israel — the Jewish People. It is important to ensure that this knot is always in place tightly against the *bayit* of the Arm Tefilin (Orach Chaim 27:2). This is because the ordinary Jew is dependent upon the Tzaddik for

spiritual insight and inspiration. The vitality of the Shechinah needed to lift people out of their spiritual fall is channelled by the Tzaddik, whose perception is so exalted that he has the power to sustain those who fall, as discussed above.

The main illumination from the Tefilin comes at the time of prayer. This is when we can attain expanded consciousness in full (see P'ri Etz Chayim, Sha'ar HaTefilin, Ch.7). This is because the Tefilin are the expression of our attachment to God, and our main attachment to God is through prayer (Likutey Moharan II:84) — both the set prayers of the fixed prayer services and one's own private prayers and conversations with God (Hitbodidut). The very word TeFiLin signifies prayer, which in Hebrew is TeFiLah.

What sort of prayer? It is written: "Wrestlings (NaFTuLei) with God have I wrestled with my sister, and I have prevailed" (Genesis 30:8). The Hebrew word for "wrestlings", NaFTuLei, is made up of the same letters as in TeFiLiN, and Rashi (ad loc.) explains the word as signifying both attachment and stubborn determination: Rachel was saying that she stubbornly pressed God with many entreaties and pleas that she should be equal to her sister Leah. "And I have prevailed" (Genesis ibid.): "He agreed with me!" (Rashi ad loc.)

This is the spirit we need in our prayers every single day. We have to persist! It takes great stubbornness and determination. Even if it seems as if your words and prayers are not helping at all, and even after days and years of trying you still feel far away from what you have been asking for, you must still carry on stubbornly. People who are obstinate do what they do for no apparent reason whatsoever. This is the way one has to be in serving God.

Rebbe Nachman emphasized the stubbornness we need in every single spiritual endeavor (Likutey Moharan II:51). Nowhere is it more necessary than in prayer, especially our own private prayers in our own words. We have to be exactly like Rachel, stubbornly pressing on, pushing ourselves forward again and again, demanding to be heard. Understand this very well if you want to achieve eternal life! It is impossible to explain everything in writing. But think of areas in your own life experience where you are stubborn and obstinate. That's how much you need to persist in your private conversations with God, even though you may often think you are just pushing on through sheer obstinacy without feeling any taste or seeing any point in what you are doing.

God "does not despise and does not abhor the lowliness of the afflicted" (Psalms 22:25) — not even when they really are despicable and abhorent! God is full of mercy at all times. There are three kinds of prayers: "The Prayer of Moses" (Psalms 90:1), "The Prayer of David" (ibid.17:1) and "The Prayer of the Afflicted" (ibid.103:1; see Zohar III:195a). These three kinds of prayers correspond to three main aspects of the Tefilin. Moses is the personification of Da'at, knowledge, and "The Prayer of Moses" corresponds to the Head Tefilin, positioned over the brain, the place of Da'at — spiritual insight and expanded consciousness. "The Prayer of David" corresponds to the knot of the *retzu'a* of the Head Tefilin. This knot is in the form of the letter Dalet, first and last letter of David's name, and is bound up with the concept of Malchut-Mashiach (see #18 above) — "The Prayer of David".

And finally we have "The Prayer of the Afflicted" corresponding to the Arm Tefilin, symbolizing Malchut, the Assembly of Israel, which is called "the afflicted" (Isaiah 54:11). The Arm Tefilin expresses the spiritual knowledge radiating in the Jewish People as a whole, and especially important is the inspiration we all need to keep ourselves from falling down completely. "The Prayer of the Afflicted" is the prayer of the individual Jew struggling to hold himself and striving to come closer to God. This is more precious than all other prayers.

The Holy Zohar describes how the poor one constantly quarrels with the Holy One, and God listens and attends to his words. When he utters his prayer, all the windows of Heaven are opened, and all the other prayers that are ascending are pushed aside by this poor, broken-hearted individual. The Psalms speak of "A prayer of the afflicted when he wraps himself (Hebrew = Ya'AToF, literally, he covers over)" (Psalms 102:1). The Holy One says, "Let all the prayers of the rest of the world be covered over (YitATFun) and let this one's prayer come before Me. We do not need a Beit Din here to judge between us. Let his complaint come directly before Me: I and he are together!"

The Holy One is directly present as the poor one thunders his prayers. "And before God he pours out his complaint." (ibid.) Before God Himself! The hosts of heaven ask one another, "What is the Holy One busy with? What is He doing?" They reply, "He is taking delight in his creatures." None of them knows what is done with the prayer of this poor one and all his complaints, but when he pours out his heart before the Holy King, God has no desire for anything else, and this prayer makes a vessel holding all the prayers in the world. (Zohar ibid.)

All this is speaking about a poor person praying for his material needs because of the pressure of physical poverty. How much more so when a person begins taking pity on himself and feels his spiritual poverty and lack of good deeds. He pleads and argues with God, complaining and thundering at Him for not drawing him closer, pouring out his words and heart until he begins crying... How very, very dear is this prayer in God's eyes: it is more precious than all the prayers in the world. For the real poverty is spiritual poverty, as the Rabbis taught: "The real poor person is the one without da'at" (Nedarim 41a). Besides this everything is vanity, for our days pass — and there is no pain like the pain of the soul, and no poverty like the lack of Torah and good deeds.

How much more so when one is conscious of enormous

debts to God, after so many sins and so much wrong-doing. There is no way of paying off the debt except through prayer and entreaty. When someone like this is aroused and begins to feel his dire straits and poverty ... when he stands before God like an impoverished beggar at the doorway, brokenheartedly appealing for his soul, begging to be saved from destruction, from the loss of both worlds... as King David said, "What profit is there in my blood, if I go down to destruction" (Psalms 30:10) ... "Save my soul from the sword, save it from the power of the dog" (ibid.22:21.) ... Certainly this prayer is more precious in God's eyes than all the prayers in the world!

Examine every single word in above-quoted passage from the Zohar and you will understand how precious are the words of private prayer we pour out before God, even though it seems as if we have been praying for such a long time without accomplishing anything. Even so, not a single word is lost: all are counted and stored in God's treasuries, even though it is quite impossible for a person to know in this life if his devotions have accomplished anything or not. Even if one has accomplished nothing but a hairsbreadth in one's whole life, this alone is more precious than all the life of this world. Even the slightest twist of a gesture one makes to come a little closer to God, even less than a hairsbreadth, sends one racing hundreds of thousands of miles in the upper Worlds (see Rabbi Nachman's Stories pp.447-51).

You must be firm and stubborn and determined about this — endlessly so. If you will persist — "Wrestlings (NaFTuLei) with God have I wrestled" — in the end you will certainly succeed in what you want and come close to God just like your brothers, the pure, the Tzaddikim. As Rachel, who had been barren at first, concluded: "I have prevailed!" — "He agreed with me!" I was so obstinate and I pressed God so much that even though I often thought my words could no longer have any effect at all, God forbid, I still pressed on stubbornly.

And in the end — "I have prevailed!" — "He has agreed with me!" I *can* be equal with my brothers and draw close to God in truth. Amen. Amen.

*

A PRAYER

Master of the Universe:

Please give me the privilege of being able to fulfil the mitzva of Tefilin properly, in all its details and with all its fine points, and with all the thoughts and intentions that are associated with it. And so let me fulfil all the six hundred and thirteen mitzvot, all of which are bound up with the mitzva of Tefilin.

Let me fulfil this holy mitzva every day with valid Tefilin made by a truly upright and saintly scribe. Let them be Tefilin written with great holiness and prepared with full attention to every detail, whether in the writing of the parshiyot, the preparation of the batim and the retzu'ot, the sewing of the batim with sinews, and everything else. Let everything be of the highest possible standard in complete accordance with all the laws of the Holy Torah. Let my Tefilin always be valid in every respect, let them be the most beautiful possible, and absolutely holy.

Let me wear the Tefilin of Rashi and Rabbenu Tam every single day. Let me place my Tefilin in their proper position on my head and arm. Let me wear them with happiness and delight, and with intense concentration. Let me be so inspired and joyous, that this awesome mitzva will bring me to the highest levels of holiness — a holiness coming directly from the supernal source of the Tefilin, which is Your own Supreme Holiness. And through this, help me to become genuinely attached to You in the strongest possible way.

When I am wearing the Tefilin, let me never lose my awareness of them or be distracted. Let me never say an idle word all the time that I am crowned with the Tefilin, the crown of the Supreme King. Let me wear them as a crown of splendor and glory, with the deepest awe and reverence, with a good heart and the greatest happiness and joy. Let me fulfil this awesome and holy mitzva properly in every respect, exactly the way You want, until I become truly bound and devoted to You at all times.

(from Rabbi Nathan's Likutey Tefilot I:38)